WHAT IS AN ANGEL?

IS VOLUME

47

OF THE

Twentieth Century Encyclopedia of Catholicism

UNDER SECTION

IV

THE MEANS OF REDEMPTION

IT IS ALSO THE

33RD

VOLUME IN ORDER OF PUBLICATION

Edited by HENRI DANIEL-ROPS *of the Académie Française*

WHAT IS AN ANGEL?

By PIE-RAYMOND RÉGAMEY, O.P.

Translated from the French by
DOM MARK PONTIFEX

HAWTHORN BOOKS · PUBLISHERS · *New York*

First Edition, January, 1960

NIHIL OBSTAT

Adrianus van Vliet, S.T.D.

Censor Deputatus

IMPRIMATUR

E. Morrogh Bernard

Vicarius Generalis

Westmonasterii, die V OCTOBRIS MCMLIX

CONTENTS

CHAPTER I

DO ANGELS EXIST?

There can be no doubt, as we shall see, that the Church teaches the existence of angels, and this is sufficient for us. The Holy Ghost guides the Church in all it tells us about the facts concerning our salvation, and the Church teaches us to pray to the angels as guardians of salvation. There are many passages in the New Testament, as we shall also presently see, which show very clearly that angels really exist.

Yet difficulties arise which must be seriously considered. At the present day it is impossible to embark on a study of the invisible world of spirits without admitting at the start that a problem of a special kind is involved. It is not only non-Christians who have doubts about such a world or deny it altogether. To many of the faithful it is one of those zones of unbelief which they allow to spread to a dangerous extent in their minds. Many go so far as to think that the Church, in continuing to teach the existence of this world of spirits, is the slave of outdated modes of thought, and they feel that we may soon have to admit that this doctrine is almost as incredible as that of creation in six days of twenty-four hours.

Such minds will not be convinced by a mere repetition of the teaching: the problems it raises must be recognized to need an answer. We must examine the nature of the difficulties. We must realize that to a large extent they arise from weakness of spiritual understanding. Thus the Christian doctrine concerning angels must be shown to express certain perceptions of the spirit which are too often clouded over or atrophied.

DIFFICULTIES FOR THE MODERN MIND

There is no need to say very much about these difficulties in a short work like this, which seeks to introduce a subject that is often misunderstood, and I need not linger over familiar ground. The main difficulties which are found in the doctrine of angels are obvious.

The scientist who refuses to acknowledge the existence of anything beyond what he can prove with certainty by the methods of science is compelled to regard every assertion of faith as dishonest. Or, if he accepts these assertions, he only accepts them as mere aspirations, based on no full certainty of the reality of their object. The well-known saying, "I only believe what I see", has immense influence at the present day, when the minds of men are habituated to the methods of science. In the sphere of belief that element which appears to be sheer mythology and to be explicable as a purely human invention, in some degree false, is plainly most vulnerable to such attacks of the scientific spirit—in itself humble and sensible. Good and bad angels are in particular open to such criticism.

It is natural for simple men and for poets to regard non-living creatures as alive; they tend to imagine mysterious companions around them. Is Baruch thinking of stars or of angels when he exclaims: "Joyfully the stars shine out, keeping the watches he has appointed, answer when he calls their muster-roll, and offer their glad radiance to him who fashioned them" (Baruch 3. 34–5). The primitive mind is not a myth, but it creates myths. Ethnologists and historians of religion, by their theories on this subject from the beginning of the century, have destroyed only what was non-essential, but they are familiar with the primitive mind, and see that angels are congenial to it, as are also genii, demons and spirits of the earth and of the air. The primitive mind is always alive in civilized man, arising from the depths for the examination of the psychologist. Angels are unquestionably among the archetypes of the dream-world, those productions of the human consciousness which always renew themselves, angels, werewolves, dragons and so on.

The scientific mind is reluctant to suppose that in the cases of possession by evil spirits in the Gospels there are really spirits, distinct from the persons of the sufferers. Usually they may be explained by our knowledge of nervous or psychological diseases. Again, Scripture attributes to the angels actions which appear simply natural phenomena, such as the destruction of the army of Sennacherib (4 Kings 19. 35–6; Isaias 37. 36; 1 Mach. 7. 41; 2 Mach. 15. 23) which we know to have resulted from a plague caused by rats, or the movement of the water in the pool of Bethsaida (John 5. 4), or the death of the first persecutor (Acts 12. 20–3). Bultmann writes:

> From the time that we have known of nature's power and laws, belief in spirits and demons has been extinguished. The stars appear to us as bodies which form part of the world, and the movement of which is regulated by cosmic laws.... Diseases and their cure have natural causes, and are not caused by the action or rather the bewitching of demons.... We cannot make use of the electric light and of the radio, or in case of illness employ modern medical methods and treatment, and at the same time believe in the world of spirits and the miracles of the New Testament. Anyone who thinks he can do so for himself should realize that, if he claims this as the position of the Christian faith, he renders the Christian message incomprehensible and impossible for our times.[1]

We must not be intimidated by these words. We shall understand to what extent they are exaggerated and excessive when

[1] *The Theology of the New Testament*, two volumes, New York, Scribners.

we have seen the place which must really be assigned to angels. We cannot explain them away. A choice between their existence and denial of their existence is inescapably forced upon us. We must examine why this is so. It is much more than a problem of tactics in apologetic and pastoral methods, as Bultmann in his final pages seems to suggest. Clever people are troubled and keep quiet about angels and devils in order, as they think, to render the Gospel more acceptable. Such opportunists try to "bring it up to date", but we should look deeper, and try to see what Scripture and the Church are really teaching about the angels. Then we should accept the teaching strictly. Let us reflect on the meaning of revelation, without being surprised at finding it surprising, since it is concerned with facts that are beyond our powers of perception. We should face what is presented for our consideration and not be upset by it. When a Christian recognizes any teaching as certainly revealed, he should get rid of any uneasiness, and certainly not feel embarrassed by it. It may be that what troubles him in the message is precisely the thing that will have a decisive influence in bringing about his salvation.

Yet it is a fact that modern man cannot think of angels with the simplicity or subtlety of the ancients. In order that faith may give him something which will perfect him and take him beyond himself, he needs first to recognize its claim upon him.

Thus we should not be afraid to see in Scripture, as far as we can, that element which is due to the very human mentality of particular ages and circumstances. It is not only the languages and phraseology of the sacred writers which condition divine inspiration; divine inspiration must also be determined by their conceptions, their sentiments and their imagery. The ray of light is broken up in the medium formed by their way of thought, and consequently we unduly simplify the question if we look at supernatural realities in a misleading way, as we also do if we deny the supernatural authority of the light or fail to recognize its true power, on the pretext that the distorting human element is manifest. To a large extent we can make allowance for this. Or we may express it by saying that the human element forms a veil before us. To reveal is to exhibit a reality, which is dimly seen through the veil. If the interpretation is sound it retains the meaning of what lies beyond the veil. Far from distorting the revelation such interpretation opens a way through the thick folds of the veil, caused by the human element. Faith has no less an object than the divine mystery. Faith is as plain in its refusal to accept what is not revealed as it is eager to witness what is really revealed.

DIFFICULTIES CONCERNING THE TEACHING OF SCRIPTURE

A main reason why we cannot accept as absolutely objective what many passages of Scripture seem to tell us about the angels is precisely that these passages make no pretence to be objective in the sense we understand the word at the present day. This is clear in the book of Tobias. This book does not profess to be history in the modern sense. Indeed in some Greek manuscripts it is classed among the sapiential books. It does not aim at relating real facts, but at arousing an appreciation of God's infinitely loving Providence, full of tender care for us. It does this so well that a reader will never lose the impression it has made on him. Improbabilities in the history or geography of its story are of no importance. Indeed they are so plain that we are warned not to understand the truth of its message in any such literal fashion. The description of Raphael's character is involved in imagery which manifestly is not matter for belief. We may fully agree that a critical mind, if it looked only at this book, would see nothing in its marvels which could give us any teaching about angels.

Light needs to be shed from the Scripture revelation as a whole, and especially from that essential element in it which provides full certainty, if we are to gain profit from this book.

With this warning we cannot fail to ask whether certain strange episodes, apparently given in Scripture as historic events, are really intended to be facts, as we understand the word, or are not rather intended to symbolize the divine presence and the help God gives. Such incidents are the camp of heavenly warriors seen by chance by Jacob on his journey (Gen. 32. 2), or the episode of Heliodorus scourged by angels. The latter story is told in the second book of Machabees (3. 24–40), where the supernatural element, mingled with the historical, sometimes takes on the aspect of the marvellous (as in 5. 2–4; 10. 29–30), since it is indeed marvellous that God should come to the aid of his people.

As to the real existence of angels, or their nature and work, mere dreams cannot of course give us clear or certain teaching. That of Jacob (Gen. 28. 10–19) can only be a way of symbolizing certain spiritual communications between God and men, and we should not necessarily conclude that the angels are ministers of these. The Lord himself is described in the same fashion; he appears to announce as an object of bodily sight what is really true only to the eye of faith, when in fact angels are not seen. Their appearance would indeed be incongruous, for it is the Lord himself who acts as heavenly messenger to communicate between earth and heaven: "Believe me when I tell you this; you will see heaven opening, and the angels of God going up and coming down upon the Son of Man" (John 1. 51).

The giving by an angel to Ezechiel of the exact plan of the temple to be built (Ezech. 40. 3), and the declaration (44–7) of the laws of the restored liturgy, are told as visions and belong to a literary form which is that of a Utopia. When we read the book of Daniel we are faced with a similar puzzle, as also in the Apocalypse of St John, which teaches us in a symbolic form in the manner usual in an apocalypse. Again, when the Lord presides at the last judgement (Matt. 13. 39, 41, 49; 16. 27; 24. 31; 25. 31; Luke 12. 8; and 1 Thess. 4. 16 : 2 Thess. 1. 7), we may ask whether we should really see in the angels anything more than imaginary figures in the great spectacle of this dread judgement as pictured by Jewish apocalyptic literature.

The Old Testament undoubtedly contains many passages in which the angels mentioned may not be personal spirits, but symbols of divine attributes or God's actions, of his plan and of his judgements (so Ps. 81. 1), of his help (so Gen. 24. 7) and of his vengeance (so Ezech. 9. 4–7). The "angels" and the "heavens" are often synonymous, and a way of referring to God out of reverence in order to avoid naming him. The more Judaism set God apart in the transcendence of his inaccessible mystery, the more it spoke of the "heavens" and of "angels". Our Lord himself, in conformity with this way of speaking, uses the phrase "kingdom of heaven" to signify the kingdom of his Father and of himself, when he instituted it on earth. When he referred to the joy "with the angels of God" (Luke 15. 10) or "in heaven" (Luke 15. 7), two equivalent expressions, it was in order to signify the joy of God himself at the conversion of a sinner. Even more clearly the "angels" or "the heavenly army" are intended to manifest the divine power. Reference to the countless number of the angels was a way of exalting the greatness of God, of stirring the heart to admire and praise him. "Heaven is of thy fashioning and the heaven of heavens, and all the hosts that dwell there" (Neh. 9. 6).

"Praise him, all you angels of his, praise him, all his armies" (Ps. 148. 2). "Bless the Lord, all you angels of his; angels of sovereign strength, that carry out his commandment, attentive to the word he utters; bless the Lord, all you hosts of his, the servants that perform his will" (Ps. 102. 20–1).

The majesty and pomp possessed by oriental monarchs

provided the imagery. The Lord is even described as having a writer in attendance (Ezech. 9. 2). Representations of Cherubim were to be seen everywhere in the east, not only at the gates of palaces to guard the entrance, or on seals or altars. They even appeared in the temple at Jerusalem: the Lord "who sits enthroned above the cherubim" becomes a stereotyped formula (thus 1 Kings 4. 4; Ps. 79. 2).

Of set purpose elements of different kinds and different origins are here mentioned together, first, because they are in fact mingled together, and also because it is necessary to make the reader realize the presence in the Bible of many references to angels drawn from different sources, obliging us to the greatest caution when we discuss what is guaranteed by Revelation. Animism, various kinds of polytheism, astral conceptions of Persia and Babylon, philosophical notions, productions of popular piety, all have a similar effect. We should notice that the Bible, even in the books which speak most of the angels, the book of Daniel and the Apocalypse, are far more restrained than non-canonical Jewish literature. This wanders into fantastic ideas, as in the book of Henoch, which tells us the names of a hundred and fifty angels, and loses itself in absurd descriptions. Philo speculates on the degrees of beings and powers.

A number of passages suggest the ambiguous character of many others, in which we cannot say whether there is reference to God himself under a symbol or to real creatures. The latter are the occasions on which, from Genesis to Judges, the "angel of the Lord" appears. Some of these passages show manifest signs of frequent re-editing. The "angel" appears to Agar in the desert at the time of her two flights, and spoke to her as God himself (Gen. 16. 7–14; 21. 14–18). He visited Abraham at the oak of Mambre and the patriarch interceded with him, that is, with the Almighty, on behalf of Sodom (Gen. 18). He stayed the arm which was about to sacrifice Isaac, and again on this occasion the promise he made was one that could be made by God alone (Gen. 22. 11–18). He wrestled with Jacob under the form of a man (Gen. 32. 23–32). He appeared to Moses on Horeb "through a flame that rose up from the midst of a bush" (Exod. 3. 2), this being the great theophany when the God who Is commissioned Moses and revealed his name. At the time of the passage over the Red Sea and through the desert he was the pillar of cloud and of fire (Exod. 14. 19). He rebuked the Israelites when they reached Palestine for having made a league with the inhabitants of the land (Judges 2. 1–5). He was a visible appearance of God, who thereby safeguarded his transcendence. Yet on several occasions he had every sign of being a creation with a definite individuality, as when he advanced, sword in hand, upon Josue and told him, "it is the captain of the Lord's army that has come to thy side" (Josue 5. 13–15), apparently like a general commanding the army of the King. This is certainly very puzzling.

Even the word, angel, lies open to a whole range of meanings. The Greek ἄγγελος, equivalent to the Hebrew Mal'ak, signifies messenger, envoy, and so representative. There are very many kinds of being, and a given function cannot tell us the nature of him who performs it. The lightning is God's messenger, or must we conclude that the angels are like fire (Ps. 103. 4)? On the other hand, the angel of the covenant who "all at once will visit his temple", must be the Lord himself (Mal. 3. 1). Christ is to proclaim himself the angel of the testament, and to cause John the Baptist to be recognized as the mysterious messenger who will precede him (Matt. 11. 10).

ANGELS UNDOUBTEDLY EXIST

Whatever hesitation may be felt about the meaning of many of the passages, there are some—in particular, passages in the Gospels—so simple and direct that we are compelled to believe without doubt that angels exist.

The appearances to Joseph only take place in dreams (Matt. 1. 20, 24; 2. 13, 19), but the angel which speaks to Zachary, and especially the angel which announces to the Blessed Virgin the Incarnation and seeks her consent (Luke 1. 11–22; 26–38), and the angels which appear to the shepherds on Christmas night (Luke 2. 9, 13), are all described with such realism that it seems difficult to deny the existence and character of these heavenly messengers without casting doubt on the truth of the Gospels.

Again, on those momentous occasions after our Lord's temptation and during his agony, Matthew and Mark record that on the former occasion angels ministered to him (Matt. 4. 11; Mark 1. 13), while Luke records that on the latter occasion an angel strengthened him (Luke 22. 43). This must be taken literally, not merely as a way of saying that divine assistance would only come supernaturally, since, between these two events, in the course of our Lord's ministry, the evangelists never express in the form of angelic assistance the support received by Christ from his union with the Father (John 4. 32). Christ himself speaks of the help he might receive from angels, but then during his passion refuses it: "Dost thou doubt that, if I call upon my Father, even now, he will send more than twelve legions of angels to my side?" (Matt. 26. 53). However broadly we interpret our Lord's willingness to express himself in accordance with the mentality of his disciples, his words are too grave at such solemn moments as these not to be taken literally. The contrast in the Gospels between the occasions when the angels appear, and the occasions when they do not appear is impressive, as we shall see, and would be inexplicable if these ministers of the mysteries of salvation were not real. We can understand the attitude taken by our Lord, who sometimes has recourse to their services and sometimes conceals it or even refuses it; no reason, however, would explain why the evangelists should invent this, at times recording the angels' intervention and sometimes not doing so, especially as they do so at a moment, the morning of the resurrection, when angels appear in a number of different ways, just as would real persons. To appreciate these details we must examine the very different accounts which are given by the four evangelists (Matt. 28. 2, 5–7; Mark 16. 5–7; Luke 24. 5–7; John 20. 12–13). I shall emphasize later how factual these details appear, particularly when compared with one another.

No less factual are the events recorded in the Acts, especially the appearance of the two angels to the apostles immediately after the ascension (Acts 1. 10), the deliverance of the apostles and of Peter by angels (5. 19 and 12. 7–11), the angel who came in full daytime to Cornelius, whom Cornelius saw manifestly, and by whom he was told to seek Peter at Joppa (10. 3–7).

Again, we must take very seriously the words of our Lord, when he speaks about the angels who protect the little ones and always see the face of God (Matt. 18. 10). No warning could be more emphatic, for our Lord would not speak lightly of the soul of a child. To make us realize the immense respect we should have for these children he surely would not be content with poetic imagery, or a fairy story. What is undoubtedly the plainest of God's declarations about angels, and that which tells us most, is guaranteed by the grave circumstances in which it is uttered, for God is speaking to men as possessing the dignity of free spirits and with reference to the souls of children.

We must take no less seriously our Lord's teaching about the devil and about devils. Many instances of possession in the Gospels may certainly be only instances of disease, and it may be that our Lord sometimes gives the impression of exorcism when in fact he is only curing diseases. But if we examine a large number of such cases we cannot explain them in this way. Our Lord simply reverses our way of thinking. Far from taking possession as a disease, in the way we do, in many cases at least he attributes disease directly to the action of devils. His conduct shows this. Thus, when he heals the sick man, a lunatic, or, as we should say, an epileptic, whom his disciples could not heal, he casts out a devil (Matt. 17. 14–18). He teaches us that the world is under the power of Satan, who is its "prince" (Luke 4. 6; John 12. 31; 14. 30; 16. 11; cf. 2 Cor. 4. 4; 1 John 5. 19), the enemy who sows tares in it (Matt. 13. 39). The redemption consists in driving out this powerful spirit from the rule he has assumed over men, and even over things, acting by means of a multitude of evil spirits. Liberation from this rule begins with a personal struggle between Christ and the devil in the desert (Matt. 4. 1–11; Luke 4. 1–13), and the climax is reached in the passion, when Christ seems conquered by the power of darkness (Luke 22. 53), though in reality it has no hold over him (John 14. 30). However puzzled we may be by such revelations, they are beyond doubt. Our Lord asserts them so clearly that we must do our best to understand them; we must not explain them away to suit our ignorance. Since every creature of God, and every work of God, is good, very good (Gen. 1. 31), we must conclude that evil spirits were originally noble and have fallen from their high estate.

The existence of angels, good and bad, is asserted no less emphatically by St Paul. From our present standpoint the most remarkable feature in the Apostle's teaching is that, being forced to react against an exaggerated cult given in some quarters to angels, it would have been easy for him to settle the matter by explaining that they are imaginary beings. He does nothing of the kind, but declares that Christ is pre-eminent over them (Ephes. 1. 21; Col. 1. 16; 2. 9). The sudden light he sheds on the true character of the warfare of this world is remarkable indeed, and entirely agrees with the Gospels. The Christian is carrying on Christ's warfare against the angels of darkness:

Draw your strength from the Lord, from that mastery which his power supplies. You must wear all the weapons in God's armoury, if you would find strength to resist the cunning of the devil. It is not against flesh and blood that we enter the lists; we have to do with princedoms and powers, with those who have mastery of the world in these dark days, with malign influence in an order higher than ours. Take up all God's armour, then; so you will be able to stand your ground when the evil time comes, and be found still on your feet, when all the task is over. (Ephes. 6. 10–13; cf. 1 Peter 5. 8–9.)

St Paul's teaching about the angels is difficult, and I shall have to speak of it again: for the moment I am not attempting to explain what Scripture teaches about angels, apart from the fact that it teaches they exist. To avoid repetition I shall only mention what it says on a few points, where it makes us look more closely. Here it need only be said that, if we look at St Paul's teaching about the angels as a whole, it is particularly difficult to solve a problem, which will occupy us throughout this book, namely, to what extent we should consider the teaching about the invisible world as due to the mentality of the time and possessing no supernatural guarantee, and to what extent the teaching is asserted by the author of the Scripture to be certainly divinely guaranteed. It is impossible, I think, to make a neat division between two kinds of basic doctrine, especially as the Apostle only speaks occasionally about the angels, and even tries to discourage an exaggerated interest in them and a false cult of them, which his correspondents ventured to indulge in, to the detriment of Christ. Nevertheless, if we look at St Paul's fundamental idea on the subject, he will be found to do far more than merely echo the belief commonly held around him. His idea is that of the faith, developed to the fullness of Revelation, recognizing in the writings of Scripture, however strange they may be, that which is derived from the teaching as a whole, as accepted by a simple mind, namely, the existence of messengers of God suddenly intervening in accordance with the hidden designs of him whose ways are not our ways (Isaias 55. 8), agents of a higher world which governs us, and draws us to him. Taking this view we have to try to harmonize two kinds of teaching, which are difficult to harmonize, on the one hand that of love, grace, personal free relationships, in which the living God, now known as Father, Son and Holy Ghost, communicates with us, his children, by personal messengers, and on the other hand, the cosmic order subject to its regular laws, in which, nevertheless, angels have a part to play. For St Paul, as for the Old Testament, angels have a relationship with "the elements of the world" and the law of Moses. St Paul asserts (Gal. 3. 19; cf. Hebr. 2. 2), as does St Stephen (Acts 8. 53) and the Rabbis, as a well-known fact the function of the angels in giving the law to Moses, while Exodus says nothing about this. If we carefully examine his teaching as a whole, it appears that St Paul does far more than give a superficial agreement to a common belief. We are forced to see a profound agreement between the ministry of the angels and the power of the Law. The Law is enforced by vital principles in the economy of salvation; it is so dominating, so essential, that the assertions of St Stephen and St Paul are a necessary expression of it, far exceeding the formulation of a belief held by others.

Consequently, we must take very seriously the existence of angels, and their function as ministers between God and the world. Now we see a fresh meaning in the passages of Scripture, which we were led to minimize when we looked at them casually. We now see them from the standpoint of a critic who was not previously alive to the mysterious relations they suggested. On two points we have experienced a significant reversal in our view. We said at first that the instances of so-called diabolic possession were only diseases, but now our Lord compels us to believe that there are diseases which result from possession, or at least are due to the influence of devils. At first we regarded the Law as given directly to Moses, but now St Paul makes us accept the intervention of angels in its transmission. In these two cases in which natural activities and divine actions seemed to give a sufficient explanation we are now led to add angelic influence. However difficult it may be to conceive, this is to be expected when once angels are really believed to exist: their action must be in harmony with their nature. Spirits cannot be experienced by the senses, and of course, if a spiritual activity affects the play of natural forces, it is hidden. That such activity really takes place is one of the principal facts revealed in regard to the angels. Many passages in Scripture will probably now acquire a new value. For example, when we read that an angel struck the army of Sennacherib, it is no longer more probable that the angel is a symbol for God's action and for a plague; it is now more probable that Scripture wishes nothing else than to warn us that an angel was minister of the divine decree by means of a plague. Such action is indeed of the same kind as those we see unquestionably at work in the Gospels, and of which our Lord speaks in all seriousness.

THE TEACHING IN THE PRAYERS OF THE CHURCH

The extraordinary magisterium of the Church has taught us officially very little about the angels. This is because neither their existence nor their function as messengers and ministers of God was denied in past times. The Church's teaching power only operates in an extraordinary manner, assisted by the Holy Ghost, against a danger of error, if the threat of error obliges it to support the faith of believers. The life of faith is normally nourished by the divine Word in the human-divine medium which is the Church. Faith works in the midst of mystery; it acknowledges the mixture of clarity and obscurity, chiaroscuro, happy in what it knows, for it is

sure that all is revealed to it which is needed for the growth
in this life of eternal life. It anxiously inquires into what it
does not understand, but is calmed by the virtue of love. "Let
us go forward in peace", says St Augustine, "in the light that
we possess, that we may reach the light which we desire to
reach." It is only in God's full light that we shall have a
complete understanding of the nature and activity of the
angels. We can catch a glimpse of it in this life, as will be
briefly suggested in this book, if we examine the ordinary
teaching of the Church and enter into the spirit of its prayer,
reflecting on what Scripture tells us in the spiritual atmosphere
of the liturgy, and of the truly traditional experiences of the
faith.

The wild speculations of false wisdom opposed by St Paul
ran the risk, as we have seen, of exalting the angels at the
expense of Christ, this being plainly contradicted by the
formula of the Nicene Creed which we say at Mass, and which
tells us that all has been created by Christ. The dualism which
constantly rears its head, especially at the most critical periods,
always runs the risk of making the devil into a divine or quasi-
divine principle of evil, rivalling God. The same Creed also
proclaims that heaven and earth and all things visible and
invisible are the work of the almighty Father. The Creed had
no need to assert the existence of angels, for no one denied
this, but it is plainly implied. The contemporary texts of the
Councils of Nicaea (325) and of Constantinople (381) show
that by invisible things we must understand angels. The
danger of dualism was aggravated in the twelfth century by
the manicheism of the Catharists and, against the reviving
belief in an eternal world not created by God, the fourth
Council of the Lateran (1215) drew up the following profession of faith in which the angels are explicitly mentioned:

"There is but one true God ... the one principle of all
things, creator of all things visible and invisible, spiritual and
bodily, who, by his almighty power, from the beginning of

time has made out of nothing each of these two creatures, spiritual and bodily, that is, angelic and belonging to the world."

The Council of the Vatican (1870) renewed these declarations in the same terms; the Council of the Lateran also explicitly defined that all the angels were created good, but that some became evil through their own fault.

It is scarcely necessary to point out that these passages teach nothing new to a simple faith, rightly based on Scripture. They are only the privileged outcome of a doctrine which includes others, these others being also guaranteed by Scripture and the ordinary teaching of the Church. The extraordinary magisterium is necessary to make certain indications quite explicit. A faith, however, which concerned itself with this alone would be extremely theoretic. The common faith of the Church, nourished by Scripture, goes far beyond any of these precise definitions.

Such faith lives amid the liturgy: it has a vivid awareness of what it believes when it reflects on the way in which it prays. The liturgy of the Church is a reality which we should take most seriously into account. It is the worship offered by Christ himself to his Father by means of his mystical body, and it gradually fits men for the heavenly city. All that we find in its essential make-up is undoubtedly concerned with the order of salvation. It multiplies, of course, into countless gestures and words which possess the wonderful variety of nature, and of nature's imagination. The purely mathematical type of mind may be unable to appreciate poetry, which makes no pretence to objective truth. Certain saints, to whom the liturgy urges us to pray, undoubtedly do not answer us exactly as their story might make us expect. Such an idea of the saints cannot be taken literally; actions of this kind have changed their meaning in the course of centuries, and it is not altogether clear now how we should interpret them—such variations are inevitable while the human-divine life goes on.

Nevertheless the human-divine life is such as to be free from error in all that concerns its highest achievement. Error of this kind would be an imposture of the lowest sort, an abuse of our confidence in what affects our eternal destiny.

Now the liturgy is nothing else, so to say, than participation in the worship which the angels offer to God. We see this particularly in the Sanctus of the Mass, introduced by every Preface as the cry of the angelic choirs, which drew the saints of Paradise and on earth to God's praise. The sculptors who were commissioned to ring round the cathedral at Rheims with angels have only exhibited to bodily eyes what faith contemplates in the celebration of its mystery. It would take far too long to describe in detail the appeal to the angels which the liturgy mingles with its appeal to God. It exorcizes children and grown-up persons who are to be baptized; it exorcizes places and things, thereby witnessing to the power of evil spirits, and begging the good angels to take their place. Every day in the evening it leads us at Compline to pray to the angel guardians who, we are told, dwell in our houses. At the close of every life it prays the angels to come to the help of the departing soul, and take it into the presence of the Most High.

Thus we are instructed very clearly to regard ourselves as engaged in a vast and fateful spiritual drama, which is not merely a struggle between conflicting tendencies in us, but is rather a struggle of personal spirits, distinct from one another and distinct from ourselves.

We can all see in ourselves three dispositions, manifested in different ways, which hamper us in grasping this revelation with absolute sincerity. First, we see in ourselves the fear, not yet dispelled, that the revelation may be distorted by a mythical element. This, too, we suspect to be mingled with other dubious ideas, falsely applied to the supernatural world —for example, the idea of heavenly armies, and angelic hierarchies. Are not these an over-simplified application to spiritual things of the social laws of this life, an attempt to give them the support of heavenly models? To surround God with a court was very natural for those who thought of him as an oriental potentate, and later, in modern times, as an absolute monarch. Fear of such distortion of the faith is healthy and right. It should keep us on the alert, provided it does not stop us from recognizing supernatural reality.

Then again, we are reluctant to admit the action of powers which are said to control this world, when the elements of the material world, intelligence and will, seem to be sufficient in their own orders. We cannot understand how these higher powers can work in the world, and we feel it would be a violence to nature if they did so. In point of fact we cannot deduce the existence of such powers from sense phenomena, as could the imagination of those who invented the myths. We can never say with Newman that it is wrong not to see them. We only assert their existence as a matter of faith. It remains for us to see, if we can, how they may fit in with material forces, and in particular how they do not infringe man's freedom, but on the contrary answer to what freedom in its essence requires.

What, however, we must above all be sure to see in its true light is the tendency to give way to fear that the doctrine is too mythical or too human, and only grudgingly to admit the existence of spiritual forces. Man has always a difficulty, in whatever degree, in conceiving the kind of existence proper to a spirit. If we were sufficiently clear-minded, we ought to admit that we suppose spiritual existence to be not much more than an epiphenomenon of matter, a phosphorescence which happens to belong to it. This is because we are unduly impressed by what conditions the action of spiritual being. In particular it is because the wonderful development of the experimental sciences and techniques habituates us exclusively to what is seen or verified by our senses. Such is the spiritual crisis, that inevitably, in the sphere of religion, our principal difficulty concerns the order of pure spirits. God seems to survive better in our thoughts, because we hope that he exists, or because he tends to become only a conventional idea. The soul may still be regarded as a principle deduced, more or less hypothetically, from human activities. God and the soul are still accepted, even though vaguely, on account of man's deepest aspirations, for man remains a spirit in spite of all the aberrations due to his mortal body. But the human spirit loses the awareness of its own sovereignty (except in so far as it controls nature by scientific techniques), and so men wonder how between God and human souls there can be pure spirits, and suppose they must be imaginary.

Consequently, reflection on what can be understood about pure spirits may perhaps strengthen our spiritual powers. The whole realm of faith, too, may thereby become real, instead of being something we just accept. If we make these pure spirits really live for us, we shall see God, who is a spirit, once more as the living God, and we shall be able to live better, in our own humble state, as spirits which, though incarnate, are yet immortal.

CHAPTER II

PURE SPIRITS IN

COUNTLESS NUMBERS

THEIR EXISTENCE IS NECESSARY

The more we are puzzled by the existence and activities of angels, if we do not sufficiently grasp what is meant by a pure spirit, the more we accept them without difficulty when we appreciate what is meant. So true is this that in the view of St Thomas it is necessary that angels should exist, nothing less than necessary (Ia, Qu. 50, art. 1).

We may perhaps be inclined to think their existence is merely fitting and be glad to substitute this view for our earlier repugnance. Yet Montesquieu, who was a brilliant empiricist and no metaphysician, can persuade us that it is not so. This charming character, in his free and lively style, wrote in one of his *Cahiers*:

> I said it was quite natural to believe there existed intelligences superior to our own. For, granting the series of creatures we know around us, and the varying degrees of intelligence from the oyster up to man, it would be most extraordinary if we formed the last link. It would always be two, three, four hundred thousand, or millions, to one, that this would not be so—that among creatures it should be we who held the first place, and formed the end of the chain. No being between us and the oyster could reason otherwise.

> (*Cahiers de Montesquieu*, édit. Grasset, p. 195.)

By this line of reasoning we do not reach a proof, but an argument from what is fitting—unless, indeed, we agree with St Thomas in supposing there must be continuity through the degrees of being (*Contra Gentiles*, 2, 9; *de Spirit creat*. Qu. 1, art. 5). But are our minds prepared to take this view?

We can put the argument more precisely, and this will afford us some comfort, while at the same time indicating the incompleteness of man's condition. Fr Sertillanges has expressed the point so well that I need only quote what he says:

> The different kinds of being are plainly arranged in an order of increasing or decreasing value, according to your point of view. Mineral, vegetable, animal, man, form the steps of a ladder. In us spirit just begins; it is active during a comparatively short part of our life. During this period it is benumbed for much of the time, ever caught in the snares of the imagination, coming to itself at moments of the highest activity, though this is liable to be upset in many ways. It seems impossible to think that nothing else happens and spirit achieves nothing more. . . .
>
> We are not spirits, any more than oxide is oxygen, or chlorate is chlorine; we are only partly spirit. Our nature lies on the border. Our intelligence stammers instead of speaking, the reasoning natural to it is like the unsteady steps of a child. The activity natural to a spirit would be intuition, that is, the contemplation of an idea, just as we see bodily things with our eyes; we can only have a vague notion of such intuition and a tendency towards it, but cannot attain it. Where, then, is true spirit, pure spirit, which acts in accordance with the law of spirit, unencumbered by matter? We can hardly suppose this degree of being and value is lacking in creation. One who believes in God would certainly find it impossible to admit such a view. God who is a spirit has had to reveal himself principally by the spirit, and not to be reduced to a degradation of spirit, to making it concrete. After all it is spirit which is the normal state of being, though we, who are lesser beings, only conceive of being as body, or under the control of body. . . .

I seek for the world of stable ideas, the world of Plato, without Plato's illusions, a world which is not the useless copy of ours but another, higher, more perfect, nearer the ideal Source. I am comforted, as a philosopher, when the Church tells me: here is your world, a new scale of being which starts from man instead of ending with him, degrees of spiritual beings reaching up to the sovereign Spirit, just as you have degrees of bodily things reaching up to body animated by spirit. These are my heavenly hierarchies, these are the choirs of angels.   (*Catéchisme des Incroyants*, Vol. 1, pp. 181–4.)

Another method is also helpful, but seems to our weak minds less profound. To be convinced of it we must have so strong a belief in spirit as to be firmly persuaded of its sway over material being. Then we shall agree that spirits must exist to govern the universe, however difficult we may find the idea. This is certainly a notion which seems strange to modern man, and I shall only venture to discuss the relation between the angels and the universe after establishing a firm foundation on which to build.

The reason St Thomas gives in the *Summa* as a proof is well calculated to reawaken in us an awareness of God and of his works. Why did God create? For the sake of his glory. What does this mean? The glory which creatures can give to God is not in God, but in them. What, then, does it give to the infinite, the absolute, the eternal? The glory of God lies in the perfection of creatures, in their beatitude; God makes them exist that they may participate in his perfections. He does this out of pure generosity; God wills his greatest glory, and this implies that he wills that creatures should be capable of becoming like him, imitating as far as creatures can his being and his activity. He is, indeed, a pure act of intelligence and will. It was not necessary that he should create, but once, out of sheer goodness, he has done so, this act necessarily involves the existence of pure intelligences, for they alone can imitate God in the most perfect way.

We conceive, of course, this necessity as within the mystery of infinite love, and this idea baffles us. It makes us come back to that concept by which we have some notion of pure spirits. Such is the goodness of God that these are certainly a succession of wonders.

PURE SPIRITS EXIST

By this word "pure" we mean that they are entirely free from matter. This is no disparagement of matter: the sin of the wicked angels is sufficient evidence that impurity in the sense of sin can be found in its extreme form in a being which is utterly incorporeal, just as the perfect holiness of Christ and of Mary show that supreme purity may be found in beings of flesh.

The profound argument of St Thomas for the existence of pure spirits removes all doubt: they exist. Their complete immateriality, however, has not been actually defined as a dogma. The distinction made by the fourth Council of the Lateran, mentioned above, between "the spiritual creature and the bodily creature", did not deal with this question, for it was directed against the manicheism of the Catharists. Nor did the Vatican Council intend to define the nature of angels, but the fact that they are creatures. I must repeat that the faith of the Church goes far beyond dogmatic definitions. For many centuries the faith has been as clear as possible concerning the spiritual nature of angels. If in the first centuries, and into the Middle Ages, it appeared to hesitate, this was due to a kind of doctrinal clumsiness. We can understand how this came about, for great metaphysical clearness was needed to distinguish pure spirit from Absolute Spirit, an angel from God. It was not until St Thomas came that the question could be satisfactorily explained, and so difficult is it for those not trained in philosophy that I can only formulate it as a note for the benefit of those who have had this training.[1]

Before St Thomas many theologians asserted that God alone is absolutely incorporeal. Tertullian said plainly: "only that which is nothing is incorporeal" (he was not, of course, speaking of God). Not only the ancients, such as St Justin and most of the Fathers, were misled in this question, but even in the twelfth century St Bernard, and indeed in the thirteenth, Alexander of Hales and St Bonaventure. Some writers added to this difficulty one derived from passages of Scripture taken in too narrow a sense. An example is the well-known episode of the "sons of God" seducing the daughters of men and begetting giants (Gen. 6. 1–2), or the manna called the food of angels (Ps. 77. 25; Ps. 104. 40; Wisdom 16. 20), or Raphael's words, according to the Vulgate: "the food, the drink I live by, man's eyes cannot see" (Tobias 12. 19), or Ps. 103, understood (like Hebr. 3. 7) as if the messengers, the servants of God—the angels—were winds or flames of fire. Now all these examples of "clumsiness" show, if we understand the mentality of the authors, as clear a realization of the spirituality of the angels as it was possible for them to have. All did their best to understand and assert that the angels were free from sensible matter; they spoke of an infinitely subtle matter, ethereal, heavenly, "made of light", or "of fire and spirit". True metaphysical appreciation, entangled inevitably in an imagination not yet tamed by metaphysics, is what we should notice in the gropings of the ancient authors, far more than their mistakes.

Later on I shall pause to warn the reader against one of the chief difficulties in this question, and to point out in this connection the wise action of the spirit. The angels are necessarily a subject which is exposed to false theories. I shall have

[1] In God alone essence and existence are identified; they are distinct in an angel as in other creatures (Ia, Qu. 50, art. 2). The immense philosophical importance of angels has been noted; this has made us find a criterion of the divine other than immateriality, and distinguish the potency which is in angels from the materiality they are free from.

to mention on several occasions fictions and dangerous speculations about them, when these are well-known or important.
Unfortunately such things specially appeal to minds which are
merely curious, and above all to people who are anxious to
find fault. But I have something better to do. One of the
principal tasks for a writer on the angels is to get rid of this
rubbish, and to extract what seems certain, when a sound
faith is allied to an honest reason. We are seeking the truth,
and we are doing so for the sake of life, that we may have it
more abundantly (John 10. 10). We seek to know the angels
as they really are, beings whose existence is of importance for
our salvation.

COUNTLESS NUMBERS OF ANGELS

Without question these pure spirits exist in countless numbers. Scripture says this again and again, from Deuteronomy
to the Apocalypse, which speaks of "a multitude of angels,
standing on every side of the throne" (Apoc. 5. 11; cf. 9. 16).
"See when God comes, with chariots innumerable for his
escort, thousands upon thousands" (Ps. 67. 18); and in Daniel:
"A thousand thousand there were that waited on his bidding,
and for every one of them, a thousand others were standing
there before him" (Dan. 7. 10). The Lord Jesus himself speaks
of "twelve legions of angels", which he could call to his help
(Matt. 26. 53), and the Epistle to the Hebrews tells us that
Christian life consists in drawing near to "thousands upon
thousands of angels" (Hebr. 12. 22; see also 4 Kings 6. 17;
Job 25. 3; Luke 2. 13–14; Jude 14).

This is what faith tells us. Now, taking St Thomas as our
guide, we can meditate on these wonders, looking at the whole
matter from the standpoint of God's infinite perfections. Plato
and Aristotle, being Greeks, saw everything in relation to the
cosmos. Plato demanded a substance apart from matter to be
the idea of every nature; Aristotle did not demand this, but

put these ideas into the things themselves, while believing in intelligences which made the heavenly spheres revolve round the earth, one for each sphere, making up only a small number. In the Christian order of things spiritual salvation prevails over the harmony of the physical cosmos, and frees itself from it: some fathers of the Church, chiefly among the Greeks, thought that the angels were the ninety-nine faithful sheep in the parable, and humanity the one which went astray; they concluded that the number of angels bore this proportion to the number of human beings. (One of the most frequent mistakes in regard to the angels comes from applying to them passages of Scripture, which perhaps do not refer to them, and in interpreting these passages in a literal sense when they are only figurative.) St Augustine and St Gregory, by different ways but equally without foundation, thought they would find the proportion between the number of the angels and that of men in accordance with the number of men chosen for heaven —an idea which, though exaggerated, had, as we shall see, an element of truth.

The approach of St Thomas is quite different. Since the glory of God is the reason for the existence and nature of angels, this must also explain their number. The perfection they have to reflect is inexhaustible, and hence they must be as many in number as they are high in dignity. Just as they surpass the visible creation in beauty, so must they surpass it in multitude. The size of the physical universe gives us some idea of the greatness of God, and more so for us at the present day who know it is beyond measurement, and seems to be expanding indefinitely. There cannot be any question of size in the world of spirits, because there is no space, and therefore it is through their number that these spirits sing God's glory. Moreover there are degrees of perfection, as we shall see, in this world of spirits, and hence, again, the more perfect they are, the greater must be their number.

The reader must judge for himself, but this line of reasoning seems most in harmony with the laws of a spiritual world, and in keeping with God's infinite generosity. Beliefs about spirits are often inconsistent and to some extent unworthy. Belief in spirits, which consists in affirming a multitude of angels, as supernatural faith obliges us to do, only seems to me to produce a coherent conception of the world, if the above considerations are kept in view and we recognize this divine principle of generosity.

"I should say", writes Fr Sertillanges again, "that, if we imagine the whole creation as an inverted pyramid with its point on our level, all the matter there is would only cover the point of the pyramid, while spirit would fill the rest to its furthest extent.... It is a dreadful thing that our vision is so contracted, whether in the religious world or in that of its critics." (*Le Problème du mal*, Vol. II, p. 64).

Roused by St Thomas, Dante contemplated in Paradise:

... a light in river form, glow tawny betwixt banks painted with marvellous spring.

From out this river issued living sparks and dropped on every side into the blossoms, like rubies set in gold.

Then as inebriated with the odours they plunged themselves again into the marvellous swirl, and as one entered issued forth another.

(Dante, *Paradiso*, Canto 30, trans. Temple Classics)

See now the height and breadth of the eternal work, since it hath made itself so many mirrors wherein it breaketh, remaining in itself one as before.   (*Ibid.*, 29.)

THE LIFE OF A PURE SPIRIT

If we are to have a deeper understanding of the knowledge of angels, we need a sound metaphysic concerning spirits. Holy Scripture tells us nothing of their nature except that they are spirits (so Hebr. 1. 14). It mentions them in connection with the missions they carry out in the world as messengers. They appear unexpectedly, and we cannot understand why we find them appearing on one occasion, and not on another similar occasion. They disappear without telling us anything about their mode of thought, or their love, or their activities. This must be because such knowledge is not necessary for our salvation. With regard to them, perhaps more than in any other matter, we are tempted to follow a false knowledge, which does not render love its due. Nevertheless, provided we are aware of the danger, we shall profit by knowing what we can about the angels. Since we are ourselves spirits, wise reflection on the life of pure spirits has a good effect in awakening us to our spiritual powers, which are too often obscured by our subjection to the senses. It stimulates us, and gives a right direction to our aspirations which are otherwise too wandering. Moreover, as we are in the flesh, such reflection guards us against crude ambitions to which the spirit is too inclined when aware of its powers and needs: to know something of the nature of angels preserves us from a false idea of angels. To quote a well-known saying of Pascal: "we create angels, but trouble comes if we create too many". What we know about spirits is sufficient to let us have a true idea about the life of angels, and thus the double advantage I have just mentioned is great. It lies with us to see that the attempt is not a rash one. Newman was undoubtedly right in saying that, if we choose, we can know far more about the angels, from the fact of our own spirituality, than we can know about animals, which are so mysterious to us. Yet this knowledge is difficult, because we are only the lowest of the spirits, sunk deep in the senses, and moreover with our powers of knowledge impaired owing to our sinful state. Here I must confine myself to giving an outline of the principal conclusions a sound metaphysic can reach on the subject of angels, explaining to some extent their significance and extent, but only arguing the matter very briefly and without technical philosophical terms. Under these conditions some of my statements must inevitably seem arbitrary.

An angel is not confined by space

It is manifestly owing to our bodies that we are in a place, and are affected by this in so many respects. Pure spirit has, strictly speaking, no parts (St Thomas, *Sent*. Bk. 1, dist. 37, Qu. 2, art. 1, ad 4): "free from every kind of quantity and position" (Ia, Qu. 52, art. 2). In so far as it can be said that angels are in one place or another—for instance, in our homes and churches, where the prayer at Compline says they "dwell" —this is because they exercise their power there. Their presence means "their application, in whatever way, of their powers in this place" (Ia, Qu. 52, art. 1), with the previous direction of their thought and will towards it.

Hence it is true to say that they change their place, either because they suddenly shift their activity from one point to another in space, or because they act at intermediate points.

An angel is not confined by time or its changes

Strictly speaking time is the measure of bodily movement; a clock is regulated according to the rotation of the earth. A spirit has its own kind of duration, varying according to its form of life. That of a pure spirit is not eternity, for God alone is eternal, eternity being freedom from any kind of duration, and consisting in full and undivided possession of oneself. Since angels live by acts of intelligence and love, which are successive and distinct, and to which they commit themselves fully, their duration is not continuous but is made up of instants which are quite distinct and disconnected, like flashes of light. Newman suggests this in his *Dream of Gerontius*:

> But intervals in their succession
> Are measured by the living thought alone,
> And grow or wane with its intensity
> And time is not a common property;

(shared with bodily movement, which always, whatever kind it is, also involves quantity).

But what is long is short, and swift is slow
And near is distant, as received and grasped
By this mind and by that, and every one
Is standard of his own chronology
And memory lacks its natural resting point
Of years, and centuries and periods.

An angel is ever free

A spirit has the double privilege of being simple and incorruptible; it never gets away from itself. Our spirit is only
partially present to itself, or to others, or to that on which it
acts, but this is due to its subjection to the flesh. Being simple
a pure spirit is wholly committed to every one of its acts;
being incorruptible it does not change when it acts. There is
no contradiction in it from moment to moment, and no altera-
tion; it is wholly and completely committed. We call to mind
Plato's words: "That which is higher has never been permitted, and is never permitted, to do anything but what is
most noble" (*Timaeus*).

It is undoubtedly in this way that we shall best understand
the scholastic theory that each angel is by itself a species:
being perfect, it has no need of other individuals to perfect its
species, but contains in itself all qualities possible to it
(Ia, Qu. 50, art. 4).

"If we had a perfect knowledge of the duties of angels, and
of their distinctions, we should realize perfectly that every
angel has its own duty and its own order in the universe, far
more so than any star, but this is hidden from us" (Ia,
Qu. 108, art. 3).

An angel knows itself perfectly

A pure spirit is open to itself, perfectly intelligible. Our
own spirits, which are incarnate, have as the object of their
knowledge that which they can understand of sensible reality,
and it is only with difficulty that we raise ourselves up to
purely spiritual reality, and we have to base the ideas we have

of it on images and comparisons, however slightly, and always starting from some object outside ourselves which we perceive with our external senses. As to knowing ourselves, each of us is the greatest puzzle to himself. To the pure spirit the primary object of its knowledge, the object best suited to it, is manifestly itself.[2] It knows itself by direct intuition, and it is in itself, through the medium of its own substance, that it knows all things, that is, God, of whom it is a perfect image (Ia, Qu. 56, art. 3) and other beings. To know the latter it requires various different ideas, which answer to them, for its essence is a likeness of them. There is nothing subconscious in it. Not long ago the angel seemed like a diamond, but now it seems like a bright crystal.

The knowledge of an angel is through the causes of things

Its knowledge is not, like ours, derived from things. It is a sign of our spirit's subjection in its present incarnate condition that it receives impressions of objects by means of the senses. A pure spirit only receives its knowledge from the Infinite Spirit. From the first moment of its creation God infuses into it the ideas of all it will have to know. This does not mean that it actually has this knowledge from the beginning, but that it is ready to consider it at the proper time. At the beginning it is fully equipped with the knowledge it will have to use. These infused, innate, ideas are directly derived from the divine model and creator of things (Ia, Qu. 55, art. 2). I quote from Jacques Maritain: "An angel knows *a priori* all the things in this world, through their supreme causes, because it knows them through a participation in the very ideas which produce them, because it knows the work of art—I mean all this universe—through the fact that the artist has communicated to it his practical knowledge, the very cause of being and of all beauty."

[2] For those who understand philosophy: the essence of the angel is intelligible in act, because it is a subsistent, immaterial, form.

We may say, then, that idealism is true of the angels: it is the philosophy which deals adequately with spirit, while its mistake is in treating incarnate spirit like pure spirit. Perhaps the most absolute idealism is true of angels, in the sense that angelic ideas are the principles necessary for the existence of things. Perhaps Platonism is true with regard to the angels. What I mean is that perhaps, in order that things may exist, their ideas may have to exist outside themselves, not only in God, but in pure intelligences, and they come into being when these intelligences think of them. Since a spirit is not, as we are, dependent on the senses, it seems far more in harmony with its nature that it should be, in the fullest meaning of the words, the reason for the things it thinks of. It seems likely that God, while allowing pure spirits to think of existing beings in a perfect way, should make their thought participate in his own creative act. This was how St Thomas conceived the matter, following St Augustine and pseudo-Dionysius (Ia, Qu. 55, art. 2; Qu. 56, art. 2, ad 4), and we should understand the cosmic work of the angels in this way. We may be suspicious of too beautiful an idea. When Kepler had shown that the movement of the stars was not circular but elliptical, Galileo stuck to the old theory because he thought circular movement was more in harmony with a star: he said that they always had an equal tendency towards and away from other things. We can get no help from Revelation, nor, as Kepler and Galileo did, from experience and mathematics, to support an idea which may be a vain dream. Fundamentally it rests on the conviction that thought, when it is genuine and strong, has an effect, as we see to some extent even in the weak and fallible human beings of this world, and not only in the Christian sacraments. If we seldom, if ever, have experience of this, it is because our thoughts are not *real* enough.

Granting what is certain concerning the knowledge of the angels through the causes of things, it follows at once that they know individual things (Ia, Qu. 57, art. 2). We can base ourselves on the existence of guardian angels, which is a matter of faith; in order to carry out their duty they must be aware of individual persons and particular things affecting the destiny of the souls they guard. It is foolish and false to suppose that a spirit is confined to universals, or that it is unworthy of it to take an interest in lesser things. An angel knows material things (Ia, Qu. 57), which are involved in an idea of material things.

To quote Maritain again: "Since divine causality and the divine ideas reach existence itself, they directly touch the individual existing thing, known comprehensively by pure intelligences, in the degree in which it receives being and, in the way in which a concrete thing with its matter, answers to the eternal archetype, as seen by pure spirit."

The knowledge of an angel is intuitive

Spirit is intuition, because it is simple. With us, it only analyses and synthesizes in order to form a judgement, and only reasons by discursive judgements (I repeat) on account of its condition in the flesh. But even then it acts by intuition, in so far as the process is not purely logical; at the beginning it must really see what it sees, and see it in the controlling principles, while at the end it *sees* the conclusion, the order of the component elements it has put together, and the connection between the conclusions and the principles. It must be able to see all this with a simple glance, which puts it together; during the process it must constantly correct errors by looking again at the objects of its discourse and the principles which throw light on them. Our whole intellectual activity is valid so far as those intuitions are valid; logical correction is necessary, but this is a process done better by an electronic brain. The more important element, the spiritual element, is the truth of the object which the machine or our reason has to deal with.

Pure spirit is not subject to the work of logic. It acts by

flashes of enlightenment, which it can cause to persist, and
between which there is a harmony to be contemplated. An
angel sees conclusions in the principles, principles in the conclusions, and it sees the essences of things. "It knows", says
St Thomas, "composite things in a simple way, things subject
to change in an unchanging way, and material things in an
immaterial way" (Ia, Qu. 58, art. 4). This must be so, because
it is perfectly simple, unchanging and immaterial. Error cannot slip in when the evidence is direct. Just as sense knowledge
cannot be mistaken with regard to a sensible object perceived
(unless the imagination distorts it), so too the intellect is
always right with regard to the essences of things: "A real
intuition," says Bergson, "is a true intuition." And St Thomas
remarks: "Either the intellect does not grasp simple essences,
and then it has no knowledge of them, or it knows them as
they are" (Ia, Qu. 58, art. 5). An angel cannot be mistaken in
the natural order.

*The knowledge of an angel is concerned with universals in
proportion to its perfection*

This may seem a truism. A spirit's perfection is in proportion to its power to have a real command over a greater
or less field of knowledge. Yet, however fine may be some
human spirits, able to understand a mass of things under a
single aspect, and with reference to the same principles, for
us the universal always gives but a partial knowledge. When
we abstract ideas from the sense impressions, we leave behind
the particular elements in the various objects. By means of
their ideas angels "grasp from a single point of view a number
of natures and individuals, each seen with their ultimate distinction. . . . By a single one of their comprehensive ideas
angels grasp the whole reality of a part of creation". (J.
Maritain.)

The order which certainly exists among the angels depends
on the degree of their intellectual power, which puts together,

by a glance that is simple rather than successive, a knowledge of reality richer than ours.

Two kinds of knowledge in an angel

The being of things can be seen either in their divine principle, the Eternal Word, or in the things themselves, in their own nature (Ia, Qu. 58, art. 6 and 7). St Augustine calls the first of these kinds of knowledge "of the morning", because it occurs in its full purity "in the glow that radiates from eternal light" (Wisdom 7. 26), even before that morning which is the appearance of things in existence. He calls the second "of the evening", because, in the words of St Thomas, "it is obscure in comparison with the vision of the Word", and, so to speak, loaded with the experience of the day lived by creation. "All beings," says St Augustine, "are known in one way by the angels in the Word of God, where dwell, eternally without change, the causes and essential reasons of their existence, in another way in themselves: in the first way by a most clear knowledge, in the second way by a more obscure knowledge, as the idea of the artist differs from the work of art. And yet, when these works are referred to the praise and glory of God, it is like dawn in the mind which contemplates them" (City of God, 11, 29).

An angel loves, wills and is supremely free

Pure spirit is pure love, and this is a wonder to us, in whom an extreme of intellectualism dries up the heart—a failing which does harm both to thought and to love. For beings have their meaning and value, precisely because of the tendency their creation has given them. Love has created them and controls them; and their perfection consists in their likeness to God. "Love moves the sun and the stars", and more still spiritual beings. The attraction of the creator, who is the source of beatitude, an attraction more general than that of gravitation, provides them with a desire for good which in early times was called will. What we at the present day call will is only a reflective, conscious choice. An angel, whose knowledge is purely intuitive, does not reflect; it sees and loves, and this love is an effective motive force. In an angel there can be no opposition between knowledge and love, and none between love and will, except in so far as an act of will serves to express faithfully the love itself.

Thus the act of an angel can be that pure expression of its inward tendency, to which we aspire in vain. It consists indeed of particular acts of will following the direction of the missions received from God, but these particular acts of will do not swerve at all from the deep demands of love. The contemplation of the angels is not interrupted thereby, because it is an understanding which is always in harmony with the truth which causes beatitude, and which controls this love and this action (Ia, Qu. 112, art. 1 ad 3).

To their knowledge through the causes of things, and to their fullness of love, there corresponds a freedom which is also supreme. With all their being they are attached to nothing less than the Infinite. They are also infinitely secure in regard to the attraction which any created reality can exercise upon them, whatever perfection it may possess. Such clear intelligences appreciate it at its true value; the love of such hearts fosters it and guards it, just as it appears to divine love, without letting it draw them astray.

The limits of an angel's knowledge

An angel is the highest of creatures. Only the secrets belonging to God alone are withheld from its knowledge—obviously, unless God himself reveals one of them. An angel can only guess the future, though in this it is far cleverer than the cleverest man: "It knows the causes of things more universally and more perfectly than we do" (Ia, Qu. 57, art. 3). What, however, depends on the will of God and man's free choice is beyond any created wisdom, for God alone is present

to that which to us is future. His eternity controls all time,
but this is not true of the duration of an angel. It "only sees
future events when they occur, but sees them from the time
that they occur.... Not being eternal, it only coexists with
things which succeed one another in time so far as these
things gradually come to pass". (Pègues.)

Nor does an angel know the secrets of hearts; these too it
guesses by interpreting outward signs. The will of man is a
sanctuary which only God's eyes can read. "For it is subject
only to God, and he alone, being the final end, can act upon
it" (Ia, Qu. 57, art. 4); in the same way he alone knows what
is hidden in the will. The same is true of the thoughts which
the angels keep secret from each other, and still more so of
the mysteries of God's actions. An angel contemplates them
in the Word, while the Word reveals them to it according to
its capacity (Ia, Qu. 57, art. 5).

The angels enlighten one another and speak to one another

The will is not the only thing that is inviolable in every
creature; the intelligence also has complete independence.
God alone is "the sun of spirits", in the noble words of
St Augustine. St Thomas agrees with this conception, in the
sense that God alone is the exemplary cause, whose image
created spirits reflect, and that he alone gives to spirits their
ultimate perfection (Ia, Qu. 106, art. 1, ad 3). But we must
follow pseudo-Dionysius, and assign to the angels a function
of enlightening one another, the higher angels preparing the
lower angels for union with the divine Word. A pure spirit
which is brighter and more powerful renders itself present to
a lesser spirit by turning towards it, exercising its power upon
it out of love, and the lesser angel is strengthened in its own
intellectual power. The higher angel through this contact
communicates ideas in the degree fitted to the lesser, awakening in it its innate knowledge. The higher angel enriches it,
too, with quite fresh knowledge, while it transmits God's

messages, adapted to its mode of comprehension which tell it of the development of plans for salvation.

Enlightenment is given by the higher to the lower angel, a strengthening and progress in actual knowledge. An angel is only said to "speak" to another when it manifests its thought to it, and this can be done by the lower angel to the higher (Ia, Qu. 107). The words are spoken in absolute silence by spirits which are at peace; the words are pure thoughts, and may be secret confidences if an angel wishes only to speak to a single other angel, and then it need only direct its thought towards this other. The words may become "cries", through the greatness of what is said and the greatness of love (Ia, Qu. 107, art 4 ad 2).

THE HEAVENLY HIERARCHIES

I have assumed that there are different degrees among the angels, and this is certainly true. Perfect order reigns undoubtedly among them; they make up a "city", "armies", "legions", and this supposes some hierarchic principle. Many passages of Scripture may be quoted in support.

The word, hierarchy, makes us think at once of the system of pseudo-Dionysius. This mysterious author of the fifth or sixth century for a long time enjoyed immense authority, being taken for Dionysius the Areopagite. It was remembered that he was a convert of St Paul himself, and St Paul must have seen the angelic hierarchies when he was carried up into the third heaven (2 Cor. 12. 2–4). Dionysius simply declared that he taught nothing of himself, but reported the teaching of saints, "who have enjoyed the sight of angels". In fact he constructed a remarkable but rigid and very arbitrary system, inspired rather by neo-Platonic conceptions than drawn from Scripture. To compose his heavenly hierarchy he combined in a systematic way names of angels which St Paul mentioned without consistency and perhaps even without meaning it literally. He gathered other names from other places in

Scripture, and from this disconnected and doubtful material built up a regular structure. This structure is so celebrated, and so attractive to some minds, that I must pause to show how arbitrary it is.

St Paul declares to the Ephesians (1. 21), in order to make clear the absolute superiority of Christ over the highest creatures, that God made him sit "high above all princedoms and powers and virtues and dominations". The Apostle is referring to the names of angelic hierarchies which were classic in the most extravagant of Jewish speculations. So too he declares to the Colossians (1. 16): "They were all created through him and in him", especially the invisible creation, "thrones and dominions, princedoms and powers". This gives the impression that the four names represent all the invisible creation. But it is quite certain that St Paul, in a lyrical passage, throws out these names without any intention of strict accuracy, and we can see that the names common to the two lists occur in a different order. Thus we have no right to base on these passages assertions about the order that should exist among the angels. Three of the five names in these two passages appear elsewhere, and sometimes in a surprising way. In Ephesians (3. 10) the principalities and powers seem to make up the whole angelic world and to depend on the Church on earth for their knowledge of the mystery of salvation. Further on (6. 12), they are among "those who have mastery of the world in these dark days, with malign influences". I shall have to explain these two passages, but the first at once confirms what I have said, that St Paul, when he mentions these different kinds of angels, does not intend to teach us about their hierarchies. Dominions and powers appear again in Colossians 2. 10, as ruled by Christ, their "head", and, all at once (2. 15), as "robbed of their prey" by Christ, "put to open shame, led away in triumph". There is another strange fact which needs to be explained. In 1 Cor. 15. 24, when Christ "places his kingdom in the hands of God", he will have first "dispossessed every other sort of rule, authority and power", which are thus treated by Christ as "enemies" (15. 25). In Romans 8. 38, "angels", "principalities" and "powers" are mentioned in a general way, and in 1 Peter 3. 22 "angels and powers and princedoms".

Archangels were known to Jewish writers, who saw in them the higher angels, "those seven who stand in the presence of the Lord" (Tobias 12. 15), to whom names were given (more than seven, as there are several variations); apart from the three who appear in the Bible, Michael (Dan. 10. 13, 21; 12. 1; Jude 9; Apoc. 12. 7), Gabriel (Dan. 8. 16; 9. 21), Raphael (Tob. 3. 25); Phanuel, Uriel, Jeremiel, Raguel and so on have been invented. If Michael was chief of the heavenly armies (Apoc. 12. 7), it would seem that he should be put in the highest rank. To the Jews he was the "viceroy of heaven". The meaning of his name, "Who is equal to God?" only applies if he is the nearest to God of all the good angels. Generally speaking, the archangels, as their name implies, are the chief angels. It is strange that they form one of the lesser degrees. According to St Paul (1 Thess. 4. 16) it is an archangel who will announce Christ's coming.

As to the Seraphim, they are mentioned in Isaias (6. 2, 6). The Cherubim are derived from Babylonian imagery; we find them set by God at the gate of Paradise after the fall to prevent any entrance (Gen. 3. 24), just as a guard is mounted at the entrance of a palace. Images of them were set up over the ark (Exod. 25. 22), and in the temple (Ezech. 10. 19), and Ezechiel saw them by the river Chobar (Ezech. 10. 20; 1. 5 following). They are not to be confused with the Thrones, for the Lord is "enthroned above the Cherubim" (Ps. 79. 2), a common expression. So St Gregory of Nyssa understands it.

We can see how confused is the account given, and so we shall be wise not to interpret the matter in a way not intended by the sacred authors. It is in other directions that we should look for an interpretation of our faith. St Irenaeus, even in his time, was impatient with speculations which only tend to distract us from what is essential: "To think that they state the number of angels, and the order of the Archangels, tell us the secrets of the Thrones, and teach us the difference between Dominations, Principalities, Powers and Virtues!" (*Adversus Haereses*, Bk. 2, 54). St Augustine wrote to Orosius: "That there are in heaven Thrones, Dominations, Principalities and Powers, I firmly believe; that they differ among themselves I have no doubt; but as to saying what they are, and in what they differ, even though you should despise me whom you treat as a great teacher, I must admit I do not know." St Cyril of Jerusalem and St John Chrysostom were also reserved (though the latter had also suggested a systematic list). St Jerome thought St Paul himself did not know all the angelic hierarchies. The preface at Mass mentions them in a very general way, by five names instead of nine, with restraint: Angels, Archangels, Dominations, Virtues and Seraphim.

Pseudo-Dionysius thought that the nine names of angels to be found in different passages in the Bible, unrelated to one another, refer to three hierarchies, each of three orders: first hierarchy, Seraphim, Cherubim, Thrones; second, Dominations, Virtues, Powers; third, Principalities, Archangels, Angels. They must be put in descending order, for the term, hierarchy, has for Dionysius a special meaning, implying much more than the mere degrees in the order of a group. He employs the original sense of the word, a sacred order set to preside over the government of the world by God, who arranges, in a descending order, that beings shall be like him. Here we have one of the great Dionysian ideas, which undoubtedly correspond to an essential aspect of things. Nevertheless he has conceived them in too narrow and rigid a way, and has in too arbitrary a fashion fixed the order of his three hierarchies.

He has been too narrow, because what is sacred must, in the Christian world, be only an aspect of the divine. Love

must have the primacy and, while Dionysius undoubtedly
thinks he has given it the primacy, his whole system, and all
he says, has an intellectualism which is not that of the Gospels.
His God is a pure transcendence, and cannot become close to
his children. The law of mediation is in his system so necessary and precise that an archangel, for example, can only have
relations with the angels or principalities, and an angel only
with archangels and the first hierarchy of the Church of mankind. The functions of purification, illumination and perfection are exercised by the higher upon the lower, lessening
progressively, so that for mere angels union with God is so
indirect that it is weakened by all these intermediaries, and
can have but little reality. Thus it can be seen why I have
called the Dionysian conception too rigid. It gives a hardness
to the order of love, as in the strictest monarchies. There can
be no doubt that it utterly contradicts what St Paul says:
"there is only one mediator between God and men, Jesus
Christ" (1 Tim. 2. 5). This principle is so essential to
Christianity that, to be genuinely Christian, to be true, every
doctrine concerning other "mediators" must agree with it,
whether we are speaking of the Blessed Virgin, of the angels,
of the intercession of the saints, or of the degrees of the
Church's hierarchy. We shall not fail to be on our guard over
the question of the angels.

At first sight St Thomas simply seems to take over
the system of Dionysius. Such was the authority of the
"Areopagite" that the arrangement of the angels in nine
orders of three hierarchies, and the principle of divine actions
in descending degrees imposed themselves on every Christian
teacher. We should realize that this respect for the authority
of Dionysius was not due to any childish conformity; it had
every appearance of an authentic source of supernatural
knowledge. There was a duty to accept everything in it which
agreed with the faith, and to interpret, as far as possible in
the full light of the faith, what could not be taken in its

original sense. Thus St Thomas believed in the division of the angels into nine orders, called "choirs", and his business as a theologian was to look for the basis of their division, especially the principle which caused the distinction into three hierarchies.

It was a question of intelligences of varying degrees of excellence. Now, the difference of perfection in spirits is seen in the degree of universality of their thoughts, provided, as I have said, this universality does not imply emptiness but real richness. The highest angels are certainly those which know the reasons of things, the divine laws of all creatures, as these laws are derived from the first, universal, principle, which is God. Then again knowledge of these and of the chief causes at work in the universe, without the power to rise to the divine principles which control them, implies, for pure spirits, a lesser degree of perfection. Finally, knowledge of the essences of things in individual beings, arranging them only in virtue of their particular causes, without understanding them from a higher point of view, is the perfection of lesser spirits. There are three degrees of universality: absolute universality, which is that of the divine essence, then that of causes which are already many, then that of particular causes (*Sent.* Bk. 2, dist. 9, art. 3; Ia, Qu. 106, art. 1 ad 6, art. 4 ad 1; *Compendium theol.* 78).

Now all the angels are ministering spirits. They carry out duties of ministering in the great work of the spreading abroad of God's love. It is in the carrying out of their ministry that they enjoy their beatitude, and thereby give glory to God. The degree of their intelligence answers to the excellence of the work they do. This view of wisdom is so important that St Thomas treats of the angelic hierarchies when he studies God's government of the universe, and not in connection with the nature of the angels. The explanation should, then, be concluded as follows. Consideration of the universal reasons of things in God himself, which is the concern of the highest angels, involves awareness of the supreme purpose of all the different angelic works. Consequently, plans have to be laid for the performance of these works, and general arrangements made, and this is the duty of the second hierarchy. The third has to carry out the work.

Thus the angels of the first hierarchy are entrusted directly with the secrets of God's government; they are his helpers, his companions in whom he trusts. They all are like his Thrones, but the Seraphim, being in more direct relationship than the others with the Spirit of Love, are "burning fires" more than the others, while the Cherubim are distinguished by their "wonderful fullness of knowledge". We must admit that this last distinction does not seem convincing; St Thomas has had to make it because he accepted a false derivation, which he received from all his predecessors, of the two names of those orders.

Still less clear is the difference between the orders of the second hierarchy: the Dominations control the Virtues and the Powers. St Thomas decides—he thinks it suitable—that to the Virtues should be reserved the ministry of the great works of divine power, miracles, while to the Powers, of course, is assigned the duty of seeing that the lesser angels receive and follow the will of the higher angels. I say all this with reluctance, because the human mind, I am aware, finds it hard to give plausible meanings to words which seem to imply distinct realities, but which really only flow from a sacred enthusiasm seeking to express itself. The four words, Dominations, Virtues, Powers and Principalities, witness to the inability of our language to express an overflowing spiritual and supernatural energy. Any attempt to make their meaning precise is bound to fail. At least it may be said that St Thomas's attempt is the most sober and, in reality, the simplest.

Even in this difficult subject he shows his wonderful sense of order; he understands the laws governing every real order of which continuity is one of the most certain. Just as he thinks it natural that the highest order should be distinguished by supreme love on account of its nearness to the Spirit of Love, and finds it admirable that the passage from the first to the second hierarchy should come about through the relationship of Thrones to Dominations, so, too, he does not fail to point out that the bond between the second and the third hierarchy is that between the Powers and Principalities, whose names show their connection.

As to the hierarchy which is nearest to us we may be able to see more clearly. Placed at the base of this splendid structure, the simple angels are not distinguished by any characteristic which can give them a name of their own. The archangels are messengers for matters more important than those usually carried out in the world by lesser spirits. Michael and Gabriel seem to us so great, and yet we do not appreciate their true greatness, since we only judge by the duties they have fulfilled in this world, whereas these are in fact exceptional. Nevertheless, they are almost the lowest in this amazing structure. The Powers are already passing out of our sight; their duty is plainly to be princes over the archangels and angels, but they have not, like the others, shown themselves in human history.

The essential difference of mental outlook which distinguishes the thought of St Thomas from that of Dionysius is that the work of mediators is never more than a preparation of those who benefit from it for *direct* reception of God's action. I shall return to this point, but here I must say something about it. The matter has already been touched on in reference to enlightenment. In all its forms the activity of the angels is concerned with nothing else than the government of the world. Sanctification, on the other hand, together with union with God which results from it, God reserves jealously to himself. God's children, with their wills which the angels can only influence by persuasion, and with their hearts, the secrets of which are inviolable, are sanctuaries where these souls are in direct and very close touch with God. The same is also true of the angelic hierarchies themselves; the lesser angels see God face to face. In the order of divine love mediators only act upon angels and men to dispose them for more personal and freer union with God, which is freer and less confined than that which the vital reaction to grace and the vision generates, and more direct and intimate.

Now that I have explained in outline the sublime degrees which rise as high above the archangels as the archangels rise above the highest of human spirits, I may repeat that it must be in conformity with the generosity of our God that his creatures increase in number as they rise in sublimity and beauty. The multitude of the lesser angels is past counting, for among them are the angel guardians of whom one is assigned to every man who has existed, exists, or will exist. Yet they are found to be near the point of the inverted pyramid mentioned by Fr Sertillanges. Above them is the vaster throng of archangels and all the other orders which undoubtedly rise above them, and St Thomas imagines that the supreme hierarchy is certainly itself more numerous than the two others together. And one angel, in its fullness of being, is as distinct from another as one universe from another.... Do we really believe in the infinite perfection of our God? Will our words, our thoughts, our ideas, ever express that which is, and that which the brightness of God's external glory is? But that transcendent being, which the works of his hands can never sufficiently praise, all his works strive to bring close to the heart of the least among us.

CHAPTER III

PURE SPIRITS SING THE

GLORY OF GOD

THE LITURGY OF PARADISE

"See how the heavens proclaim God's glory" (Ps. 18. 2). There are different kinds of glory. Creatures give glory to God in so far as they are what he wills them to be. This glory which he finds in them for their delight is only a beautiful reflection offered to the infinitely more mysterious glory of God's personal life. The fire which crowned the mountain and the cloud into which Moses climbed (Exod. 24. 18), the radiance left upon his face, such that men shrunk from approaching him (Exod. 34. 29–30), the thunder, lightning and storm, are feeble signs of the glory which shines on the face of God himself.

The "heavens", made up of the countless numbers of angels, sing his glory in a different way from the stars, the immense galaxies, or our souls here on earth, for the angels, like the saints of paradise, *see* the glory praised by their song.

What can we say, or imagine, or think, which will give any notion of paradise? Yet we need such a notion if we are to have any idea of the principal office of the angels. For it is certainly their principal office to sing the glory of God. If we leave that which changes, and the deceptive values of what is corruptible, we are lost in emptiness. This is a serious matter, since our present life should be inspired by love of paradise. In order that this obscure instinct should be effective in us who are aware of things, it must be supported by some awareness capable of stirring up our desire. That the outcome of our lives should be to sing canticles throughout eternity, and listen to those of the angels, leaves us puzzled. Yet the instinct for paradise is an obscure awareness of God, inspired in us by his grace, and, since God is love, all that is of God, or relating to God, will have meaning and attraction as soon as we understand it in the light of love. Deep within us we have an experience of paradise. Whenever, in spite of so many obstacles within us, and obscurities arising from the world, we can make surrender of ourselves, our heart enters heaven, and knows what is meant by singing God's praise. If we renew our vigour at the most secret and intense moment of this experience, we shall understand the meaning of what Scripture and the saints tell us of the angelic liturgy.

The angels form a festal gathering (Hebr. 12. 22–3). Contemplation of "the fullness from which all beauty is derived" (Dionysius) is a joyful act for beings whose love knows its fullness. The cry which Isaias, St Luke, the Apocalypse and the liturgy of the Church put in clear words is the thrill of well-being beyond expression, which is ever renewed in the angels, because they come back to the source of their existence. It is a thrill of life, because God is their source, and they are in harmony with him throughout their being; it is a thrill eternally renewed because God is infinitely more than their source and their beatitude.

All the angels participate in the life of the Father, Son and Holy Ghost, life of their life, but infinite life through which these finite creatures are raised to ecstasy, creative life creating again and again without end, and ever giving fresh life, with a thrill which carries them beyond themselves. Their awareness of what God is, an awareness alive with a twofold life, which is that of God and of themselves, is so deeply theirs and so sublime that it is in truth rather silence than a song of praise. But how are we to conceive a silence so full of life? Far from being a dull absence of noise, we, who cannot know it as it is, can only express it as song. It is not a song with words, because it is not discourse but a burst of intuition. "It is", says St Gregory, "the movement of admiration, in which the angels are raised on high" (quoted by St Thomas, Ia, Qu. 107, art. 3). If human ears could hear it, they would be aware of it as a melody sent through space through the joy of these high places. If our hearts were not cowardly, but dared, in union with the angels, to exult in the living God, the chant of our Alleluias would be an echo on earth of this song, of this angelic silence. We know how the solemn music of the Gregorian chant breathes the joy of our citizenship in God's light.

It was necessary that our prophets should tell us something we could understand, yet in some measure expressing the unspeakable joy of this song. Being for our good it puts under different forms that which affects us; there must indeed be reference to us in this song of praise, since it is the order of our salvation which the spirits sang. Isaias heard the Seraphim cry to one another: "Holy, holy, holy, is the Lord God of hosts; all the earth is full of his glory" (Isaias 6. 3). The living figures of the Apocalypse "day and night cried unceasingly, Holy, holy, holy is the Lord God, the Almighty, who ever was, and is, and is still to come" (Apoc. 4. 8). In the night at Bethlehem the song of the angels could be heard: "Glory to God in high heaven, and peace on earth to men that are God's friends" (Luke 2. 14). We too have a part to play, and offer up our prayer at Mass, to join the song of the angels, repeating the words revealed by Isaias. Our *Dominus Deus Sabaoth* is the Lord of the heavenly armies, the God adored by the angels. It is sad that no words of ours can express the reality of the Absolute Being, utterly unfathomable, who gives himself unceasingly to the angels and the blessed, to be known in

the intimacy of his love. "Lord" has become too familiar to
us: "Yahweh" is too archaic, and conceals still more the
meaning of the Hebrew: "He is", absolute being. Not only "is
he" in himself, but he comes to us.

"God has given these, his hosts, the strength to stand firm
before his glory" (Ecclus. 42. 17, Confraternity version,
according to the Hebrew). This consuming fire does not consume his creatures, those at least whom their love, welcoming
his at the time of trial, has made like him. He is not less
terrible in himself. The wonderful security, indeed the tender-
ness, which the angels and the blessed find in him, are by no
means an easily-won delight. The joyful adoration of the
angels carries with it awareness of their essential weakness
before the utter holiness of God, a distress described in the
book of Job: "In his own retinue God finds loyalty wanting"
(4. 18). The brightness of his glory renders all things more
intense; it is in proportion to God's mystery: without measure,
even for the highest angels whose life is caught up by it. We
imagine their feelings as symbolized by the beating of the
cherubim's wings in Isaias (8). We may picture the angels as
moths madly beating with their wings against the glass of the
lamp at which they would burn themselves.

> It is nothing wonderful that God should be strange to men
> who have never seen him, seeing that he is also strange to the
> holy angels and the souls who see him; for they neither can
> nor shall ever see him perfectly. Yea, even to the day of the
> last judgement they will see in him so much that is new in his
> deep judgements, in his acts of mercy and justice, as to excite
> their wonder more and more. Thus God is the strange islands
> not to men only, but to the angels also; only to himself is he
> neither strange nor new.
>
> (St John of the Cross, *A Spiritual Canticle of the Soul*,
> Stanza 14. Translated David Lewis.)

Let us no longer conceive the angels as figures in a
spectacle, part of the decoration, flattering a transcendent

vanity. Nothing is more fundamental than Being, Spirit and
Love, and so we can see the value of the friends of him who
is infinite Being, Spirit and Love.

PRAISE OF CHRIST

The worship offered by the angels to God includes of
course worship of Christ, and especially refers to what we
call "the heavenly sacrifice" (the phrase is not quite accurate
theologically). St John heard the praise offered to the sacri-
ficed Lamb (Apoc. 5. 11–14). Christ is indeed the head of the
angels as of all the city of glory or of grace: "In him all
created things took their being, heavenly and earthly, visible
and invisible; what are thrones and dominions, what are
princedoms and powers?" (Col. 1. 16).

As "it was God's good pleasure to let all completeness
dwell in him" (*ibid.* 19), pure spirits adore him. Their natural
superiority to man can be no hindrance to their adoration of
the Man-God: "He is the fountain head from which all
dominion and power proceed," says St Paul (Col. 2. 10).

On the subject of this headship, which is certainly that of
Christ in relation to the angels, theologians have disputed
for several centuries. Since Christ has not merited grace and
glory for the angels as he has for us through his redemptive
Incarnation, the question has been asked what exactly is
bestowed by him. We know the famous words of Bossuet,
when he said that Christ is "more our head than theirs". I
cannot enter here on this difficult problem. In whatever way
Christ acts upon the angels, the chief thing is the attraction
he exercises upon them, their movement towards him, their
adoration and service.

Yet St Paul and St Peter, when speaking of the relation
between Christ and the angels, use phrases which surprise us,
and seem to imply an intense humiliation which Christ has
inflicted on them, as though on rebels (Ephes. 5. 9–11; Col. 2.

14–15; 1 Pet. 1. 12; 3. 22). It will be better to explain these words, as far as they can be explained, in the next chapter. Nevertheless, we should recall them, when we reflect on the angels' adoration of Christ, because they seem to cast a shadow on it. The impression is quite false. If Christ "led away in triumph" even the good angels, if he "robbed them of their prey", if he will "dispossess" them when he places his kingdom in the hands of God his Father, these strong expressions can only refer to the character which men falsely attribute to them; they themselves have not encroached on Christ's power. Plainly the good angels exult when they contemplate the mystery of salvation (cf. 1 Tim. 3. 16), and see themselves "robbed". Christ and the angels must be intimately joined in heaven. On earth they have shown us their joy at the Incarnation (Luke 2. 13–14), and we see how they hasten to minister to him after the temptation (Matt. 4. 11), and to strengthen him at his agony (Luke 22. 43).

This mystery reaches its deepest point, where grace most signally triumphs over nature, in the fact that Mary is given to the angels as Queen: a simple human being is higher than all these marvellous spirits. It is true that even in the order of nature the divine motherhood is so closely linked with the hypostatic union that the angels, in praising the Blessed Virgin, do not praise the supreme triumph of grace alone; they find it *natural* that she should be raised above them. Dante says to Beatrice:

> Look now upon the face which is most likened unto Christ, for its brightness, and no other hath power to fit thee to see Christ.
>
> I saw rain down upon that face such joyance (borne on the sacred minds created for flying through that lofty region),
>
> that all which I had seen before held me not in suspense of so great marvelling, nor showed me so great semblance of God.
>
> And that love which first descended to her, saying, *Hail Mary, full of grace*, now spread his wings before her.

The divine canticle was answered from every side by the blest Court, so that every face thereby gathered serenity.

(*Paradiso*, Canto 32, trans. Temple Classics.)

THE PRAISE OFFERED BY OURSELVES AND OTHER CREATURES

The liturgy of the angels obviously has the importance of according understanding and love in full perfection to the praise which rises from all creation to the three divine Persons, to Christ and Mary. As I have said, creatures give glory to God just in so far as they are in conformity with what God wills them to be. Hence beings without freedom give a worship to their Creator which is not of great value. Excellence is derived from the free action in which the creature with intelligence perfects itself through love in accordance with the divine order. In this way, as lesser creatures must do, we assign to them their meaning: let us look also at their value and spiritual tendency towards God. At the highest point of creation the pure intelligences, which are pure love, give its full meaning to the praise offered by the universe: full, because they embrace it in its entirety, and because the angels with all their free perfection devote themselves to awareness of beings and to the offering of them to God, just as the brute creation without freedom possesses the perfection due to its being. Spiritual creatures, such as ourselves, have as their duty to act as "priests" of creation, in a broad, non-sacramental, but yet a real and sublime, sense.

The angels have of course carried out their office from the beginning of the world.[1] God laid the foundations of the earth,

---

[1] I shall not pause to discuss the question when the angels were created, for it is one of vain curiosity and indeed insoluble. Some have argued from Job 38 that they existed before the creation of the material world. Others think the creation of spiritual and corporeal beings took place at the same time, on account of the words, "tota

when "all the morning stars sang together, all the powers of heaven uttered their joyful praise" (Job 38. 7). Into this picture must be fitted what I said at the beginning of the last chapter about the necessary being of the angels: from the moment the world existed perfect spirits were needed to give it its perfect meaning, which is praise of the divine glory. They alone among mere creatures contemplate the essential glory of God, so far as creatures can, and render to him perfectly the glory derived from their correspondence with his wisdom and love.

Some psalms (especially 28, 102, 103, 110, 135, 137, 148), the canticle *Benedicite* (Dan. 3. 31–90), and the liturgy of the Church express this great truth most wonderfully. That is to be expected, for the praise offered by religion on earth gives form to the action of mankind as "priests" in creation, and appeals to the angels for assurance of heavenly approval. As to the liturgy of the Church it, too, is this praise, offered by "the one mediator" (1 Tim. 2. 5), the one Priest, Christ, who sums up every order of being. In this spirit we must sing the *Sanctus* of the angels and the *Gloria* which they intoned at Christ's birth. The whole liturgy should be inspired with this spirit.

The liturgy of St James introduces the *Sanctus* in the following way: "The heavens, and the heavens of heavens, praise thee, with all their power, as do the sky, the moon, and the whole choir of stars, the earth, the sea, and all they contain, and the heavenly Jerusalem, the assembly of the first-born who are inscribed in heaven as citizens, the spirits of the just and of the prophets, the souls of the martyrs and of the apostles, the angels, the archangels, . . ."

---

simul", used by the Lateran and Vatican Councils. But these words only mean: as part of a single plan, and repeat Ecclus. 18. 1, translating the Greek which means, "all without exception". The question was much discussed when the days of creation in Gen. 1 were taken in a strictly literal sense.

THE PRAISE OFFERED BY THEIR MINISTRY

There are two elements which give the angelic praise its worth, for it is in some sense identified with the ministry carried out by these "messengers", and it gives permanence to their self-dedication, which was meritorious in the highest degree.

We are compelled to confine to particular times the acts of worship we render to God, the celebration of the liturgy, the prayers which are suitable to us, and particular acts of devotion. The angels contemplate unceasingly the face of God, and thus in their very acts of praise to God they carry out their missions. The glory they give him, when they cause the power of their wills to descend upon the beings on whom they act, increases the glory of the praise they raise up before him.

We can most truly apply to this intelligent and utterly faithful ministry what St Jerome says of the "praise" rendered by the stars, which never fail to perform their office: "The ministry itself is praise." Claudel, too, on the subject of the angelic ministry, which ever serves to make more universal ideas fitting for lesser intelligences, or to apply to particular effects a power which can spread without limit, makes the profound remark: "Service of God consists in holding him within one, keeping (*servare*) him, applying the power of the general to the particular: in fully accepting what he gives in accordance with the arrangements or plans established by Providence, in fully granting what he demands." (*Présence et prophétie.*)

A difficulty should here be mentioned which we may find in St Thomas's magnificent conception of the angelic hierarchies. He does not think that the higher angels, from the Seraphim to the Dominations, are ever devoted to an "external" ministry, such as involves "movement" to a determined place (Ia, Qu. 112; *Comm. in Heb.* 1, 14). The Apocalypse certainly seems to suggest this: the four living figures, which are certainly higher angels, do not themselves descend to the earth, they send the four fearful riders (6. 1-7). Yet elsewhere we have the impression that angels of the first rank are themselves sent to accomplish missions on earth. This is the interpretation of most scholars. It is puzzling that the seven angels are not in the highest rank. We have seen that the system of St Thomas can be so looked at that they are only in the last rank but one, yet it is strange. The difficulty is, I think, insoluble with regard to Michael, to whom the Apocalypse assigns the dignity of chief of all the good angels in the struggle against the Dragon and his angels. Why has he only the rank of archangel in the hierarchy of Dionysius? Undoubtedly we must attribute a great deal in all this to imagery, and we cannot tell exactly what is revealed. But the whole idea of the ministry of the angels is threatened, and that is why I must pause for a moment. According to the principles of St Thomas concerning the "mixed life."[2] there is no reason to think that actions applied to events in space and time may not be performed by the highest angels. They have the power for this, it would not be unworthy of them, they would be no more distracted thereby from their contemplation and pure praise than when they pass on to the lesser angels supernatural knowledge, permitting them to act upon those lower still. Nevertheless, in his theory of angels St Thomas has kept some of the ideas of social classes of past times, making the higher angels an aristocracy which only communicates with God and with the angels below them. This rather rigid feature, in no way necessary, is due, I think, to the excessive respect St Thomas felt obliged to pay to the pseudo-Areopagite. He only corrected the system on points which seemed to him to involve unacceptable notions.

However this may be, the ministry carried out by the angels, in all its forms, certainly adds to the value of their liturgy.

[2] I shall speak of this "life" in the last chapter.

HEROIC GIFT OF SELF-SURRENDER

Fundamentally the value of their liturgy depends upon the act which fixes choice permanently, and a choice was open to grave risk.

Beatrice describes the angels as follows to Dante:

> Those whom thou seest here were modest to acknowledge themselves derived from that same Excellence which made them swift to so great understanding;
>
> Wherefore their vision was exalted with grace illuminating, and with their merits, so that they have their will full and established
>
> And I would not have thee doubt, but be assured that 'tis a merit to receive the grace by laying the affection open to it.
>
> (*Paradiso*, Canto 29, trans. Temple Classics.)

It cannot be denied that the angels have been subject to a test, so severe that many of them have failed, and here I must speak about this: their state of self-surrender to God, which is nothing else than their praise of him, if it is now necessary for the attraction of God's glory, fixes for ever a gift which was heroic.

We men on earth are unstable for two reasons, because we are subject to the changes of time, and because we are full of contradictions within ourselves. Our pure gold can change into worthless lead. In any case, we are subject to the law of time, and need all our corruptible life to ripen within us the seed of glory. Pure spirits are perfectly simple and freed from time. The one act which was heroic on the part of the good angels before their entry into glory brought them to it immediately, and it has become their act of praise for ever.

There could be no doubt that this act was required of them, even if Scripture did not tell us that some of them refused and became devils, for God cannot be God and the source of happiness to spirits, which are free beings, except in proportion to the free gift by which they have committed themselves to him. A spirit must bring about its own perfection and fit itself for beatitude, by its own personal act. It is with this in mind that we must interpret what is called "merit".

That some angels have sinned is explicitly recorded in the New Testament (2 Pet. 2. 4; Jude 6), and it is also implicitly revealed, because God has created all things good (Gen. 1. 31), and yet there are evil spirits. Again, the fourth Council of the Lateran (1215) defined against the Catharists: "The devil and other devils were created good by God in respect to their nature, it is of themselves that they have become evil" (Denzinger, 428). Of the number of devils in proportion to good angels we know nothing (that the tail of the dragon in the Apocalypse, 12. 4, "dragged down a third part of the stars" is not sufficient evidence that a third of the angels sinned).

What is important is to understand what this sin was, for only in this way can we find out what test the good angels underwent, that is, the real nature of their merit then, and of their glory and praise now.

First, we must recognize that they did not enjoy the vision of God at the first moment of their creation. We always tend to think that our bodies alone prevent us from seeing God, and that a spirit necessarily sees him. But this is not so, for a created spirit is by its nature to an infinite degree unlike the Absolute Spirit. God has to grant it a sublime quality which enables it to have the vision, what is called the "light of glory". This vision irresistibly attracts every creature, so as to exclude all choice with regard to God. Some angels sinned, because they were free to grant or to refuse their love to God, and because they were not yet in glory, and did not yet enjoy the Vision.

Why, it may be asked, did not God give them this glory from the first; why did he permit the danger of so many terrible falls, which in fact have occurred? If the reader reflects, he will find I have already answered this difficult question, but I will put it in different words. A spirit is essentially a free being; in order that the vision of God shall be its supreme act in which it finds its beatitude, this act must be due to a vital process in it, freely produced. But how can a free being produce an act which is truly its own, unless it does so of its own free choice? What I mean is that a creature can have no glory, unless it previously has merit. Now glory would make such merit impossible owing to the necessary attraction it caused. The vision of God is only beatifying when won by a personal act. The spirit must rise to glory, without compulsion, by its own spontaneous movement. Such is the dignity of a free being, and it involves a corresponding danger.

Nevertheless, without God's help a spirit is incapable of meriting its glory: there is a measureless chasm between it and God, and God alone can bridge it. Hence, if the angels did not receive glory from the beginning, they had need of grace. This gave them a tendency towards God's inward life to which they were destined, and towards the whole order of salvation of the spiritual creation, in which they were called to play a part—a world as mysterious to them as it is to us. The danger these spirits incurred was that the mystery should cause their downfall. It is precisely over this that some spirits failed, while others achieved supreme excellence. We can see how hard it was for them all, for a spirit is so made as to understand its own conceptions, and itself. When the occasion arises for it to make a decision, it does so only through knowledge of the causes of things. It wills that thought and action should of themselves correspond to its principles. Thus its temptation is self-sufficiency and, in its own order, it can be self-sufficient. For it the great proof is self-surrender beyond its own direct sight, submission to an order which it cannot explain by its own powers.

The Mystery of God and of salvation was beyond them. They could continue to know God only as they knew him by the power of their wonderful intelligences, as the author of their own perfection and of that of all other creatures. Absorbed in their own excellence, they might well recognize that the revelation came from God, and yet be able to ignore it. If they were willing to throw themselves into the abyss of God's personal life and of the workings of his grace, they gave up their self-sufficiency, lost themselves in a movement of pure and simple trust in God's word.

We can see, then, what for pure spirits as such is the meritorious act of beatitude and what is sin: the former is at root pure confidence in God, looked at as perfect mystery, beyond what they know of him, the latter is pure will to be a law to themselves.

Under these conditions sin is "pride". This word is often misused to express any exalting of oneself. But it should be kept for this utter malice, this refusal of God's transcendence, in the sphere of personal and vital relationship with him. God alone, and not even his angels, as I have said, knows when we are really guilty of this. The malice of the devils is especially open in his sight. Being quite natural, it gives a very different impression, I think, from the words of Isaias: "What, fallen from heaven, thou Lucifer, that once didst herald the dawn?... I will scale the heavens (such was thy thought); I will set my throne higher than God's stars... the rival of the most High" (Isaias 14. 12–14).

Why should he desire such excellence? Unlike a tyrant, a pure spirit does not outrun reasonable ambition in wishing to be supreme in creation: it is fully aware that this is the place it has. To be like the most High is not, in the natural order, an absurd pretension for it, it is indeed God's glorious image. The folly of the devils lay in setting limits to their wisdom, "in putting the ultimate happiness in what they could gain by their natural power, and in turning aside their desires from supernatural happiness which they could only receive from God's grace". (Ia, Qu. 63, art. 3). This was a kind of "avarice" (*ibid.*, art. 2, ad 2), seeking in a general way natural goods, as wicked as pride, because the natural order does not really suffice. In reality God, the Creator, is the Trinity of Father, Son and Holy Ghost, and therefore there can be no full knowledge of God except through the revelation of this Mystery. A spirit can only perfect itself, if it passes infinitely beyond itself. What the devils failed to take into account was the revelation, which God's mercy made to them, of this need to pass beyond the natural order, by which alone the natural order could have meaning and value. Their sin was "disobedience" in a much deeper sense than failure to obey a particular command, for it consisted in the refusal to enter into the higher order to which they were called. God gave them no other command. Their "we will not serve" did not even need to be formulated in this way; it consisted in their refusal of love that alone would have supplied for their inadequate understanding of the Mystery, which was enjoined on them by the fact that God is love. God is the "order of charity". It is only possible to pass from their own order, which is also ours, "the order of spirit", by having the disposition of a servant, and becoming a child. Fundamentally, therefore, they were guilty because they did not love. When God called them to it they should have made this act of pure and utter charity, the grace of which would have enabled them to rise beyond themselves, and which would have put them at once in the state of glory.[3] In my opinion they committed themselves to their own self-sufficiency in a purely natural fashion, and hence, in relation to the order of supernatural love, their self-sufficiency took on a character of utmost gravity. When once the primacy of divine Love has been revealed, a satisfaction of self which refuses to go further cannot be maintained or be sufficient. To keep one's centre of

[3] Theologians dispute about the quality of the love which the angels possessed between their creation and their final choice. It is one of the most difficult questions of theology, and it is impossible to give a true idea of the question without a technical study, which needs theological training. Cf. J. Maritain, " Le Péché de l'Ange", *Revue thomiste*, April 1956, pp. 197–239; Ch. Journet, "L'Aventure des Anges", *Nova et Vetera* (Genève), April, 1958, pp. 127–154.

gravity in oneself, when everything is full of life around one, and when there is a duty to pass beyond oneself, is nothing else than to fall. Thus the apparent exaggeration of the words of Isaias is justified. Our Lord, too, confirms them, for he sees "Satan cast down like a lightning-flash from heaven" (Luke 10. 18). The devils fall into a state of anger and despair, and hence are necessarily at war. Since they cling to the natural order when the free love of God would take them beyond it, they become disturbers of the natural order itself.

Before the moment of their choice, all the angels were conscious of themselves, and saw themselves as God's creatures. They started, then, with a knowledge "of the evening". Called to intimate union with God, those which remained in themselves became "darkness", while those which answered with love found themselves at once enlightened with knowledge "of the morning", and were ablaze with "the praise of the Word" (Ia, Qu. 63, art. 6, ad 4). We need not be surprised that a single act was enough to establish them in Truth. We have seen that this possibility results from the independence of spirit in relation to time, and of its simplicity, and I must repeat this. We, too, who are spirits can by a single act merit eternal happiness, or can destroy ourselves, if we commit ourselves wholly. We cannot judge as to the degree of our committal, but we must, when we reflect on the angels, realize our grave responsibility. We must approach our destiny as spirits. St Gregory says that the sinner, if he really commits himself to his sinful act, "sins eternally", for it is an immortal creature who commits himself. The intensity of a pure spirit's act manifestly is beyond our power of conception; there are no half-measures for it, and no recovery. It determines itself in a flash.

THE HIGH STATE FROM WHICH EVIL BEGAN

We see, then, what sublime self-surrender determines for ever the angels' praise of God. Since this liturgy is the fruit of their test, it has a character which I must now make plain.

Clearly it involves a movement of boundless gratitude, in proportion to the danger that has passed. Like the blessed the angels see what we with so much difficulty believe. While their choice was wholly free, grace was supreme, while their freedom was perfected, it owed this to grace, indeed, with its personal self-determination. Although the angels have not sinned, as we have, their praise also is that of those who possess grace.

Nevertheless, with regard to the grace which they have been given and the glory it has won them, they must experience a very different feeling from that of the saints, who have been fully pardoned for their sins and healed from their spiritual "wounds" (which perhaps remain changed into marks of honour). The angels did not wonder at their being preserved from the evil from which the Immaculate Virgin was preserved by a special gift, for they were not preserved from any fault in nature.

There is no doubt something which adds to the simplicity of their actions, namely, that their degree of glory corresponds exactly to their natural position. With us a person of ordinary natural powers can be raised high in the order of grace. If such a person let grace do what it willed in him, he would cease indeed to be ordinary, but this would not give him the natural intelligence or artistic gifts or charm which he lacked. On the other hand, some persons of natural genius will only just manage to save their souls and will remain for eternity saints of small degree. This is because we are too complex, burdened with or blessed with a thousand chance influences, the effects of which God corrects in the supernatural order. In the angels, which are perfectly simple, nothing can be found to upset the perfect harmony of their nature and supernatural gifts. They make up a world in which excellence always has its due result. We can imagine what this could do in psychology: the infinite calm of beatitude is a wonderful thing.

Their activity, however, is not spent only in casting themselves into the divine glory, but also in so far as, by experiencing the danger they have escaped, they have realized a tendency in themselves which might have led them to sin, and have experienced in themselves the ultimate cause of all sin. They have personal knowledge that this cause is spiritual. We ourselves always lay the blame on the flesh, or suppose that sin is due to our being creatures. Our spirit is reluctant to admit its own responsibility. Pure spirits certainly recognize clearly in the creaturely state the root possibility of sin. It is plainly through their deep awareness of being creatures that they raise up their praise of God, while the Church on earth also gives to its whole liturgy the character of an appeal to the Creator to save his creatures from sin. But it is through its spirit that the spiritual creature falls. The angels know, too, that the flesh is not necessary for this. Their liturgy is that of beings who live in that region, from which evil started.

Finally, their ministry, which is a form of their praise, is marked as a result of this experience with a stronger character of mercy. They bless God's mercy for not having joined these cruel powers, against which they protect "the destined heirs of eternal salvation" (Hebr. 1. 14).

At these spiritual heights where the original drama was played, let us raise our hearts in peace. This peace cannot change: "in uninterrupted contemplation of God's will" (2 *Sent.* dist. 11, art. 5), "fixed where true joy is",[4] the angels cannot sin.[5]

[4] *Ut nostra fixa sint corda ubi vera sunt gaudia,* a phrase repeated in several prayers in the Missal. Should we translate: "that our hearts may be fixed where there are true joys", or "where joys are true"?

[5] I must mention the fantastic view of Origen, condemned by the Council of Constantinople in 543, according to which the whole spiritual world is ever unstable, the good angels being able to fall by taking bodies and committing sins of the flesh, human souls being fallen angels, and men being able to become angels again or fall amid the devils.

Dante looked at Paradise as a huge white rose, made up of "people old and new"—those of the Old and of the New Testament—and on that rose another people, the angels, gathered:

But the other, which as it flieth seeth and doth sing his glory who enamoureth it, and the excellence which hath made it what it is,

like to a swarm of bees which doth one while plunge into the flowers and another while wend back to where its toil is turned to sweetness,

ever descended into the great flower adorned with so many leaves, and reascended thence to where its love doth ceaseless make sojourn.

They had their faces all of living flame, and wings of gold, and the rest so white that never snow reacheth such limit.

When they descended into the flower, from rank to rank they proffered of the peace and of the ardour which they acquired as they fanned their sides,

nor did the interposing of so great a flying multitude, betwixt the flower and that which was above, impede the vision or the splendour;

for the divine light so penetrateth through the universe, in measure of its worthiness, that nought hath power to oppose it.

This realm, secure and gladsome, thronged with ancient folk and new, had look and love all turned into one mark.

O threefold light, which in a single star, glinting upon their sight doth so content them, look down upon our storm.

(*Paradiso*, Canto 31, trans. Temple Classics.)

CHAPTER IV

MINISTERS OF MERCY

THE ANGELS IN THE CHRISTIAN ORDER

A true idea of the ministry carried out by the angels among us depends on having an accurate idea of their place in the order of salvation. An important question arises here: has not the coming of Christ deprived them of all their duties and even of all their dignity? We must now consider the strange passages of St Paul and of St Peter to which I alluded in the last chapter.

Two of them seem to imply that the angels could have been kept in ignorance of the mystery of the redemptive Incarnation, in such a way that it is through the Church, carrying on the mystery among us, that they would now have the revelation. St Paul writes to the Ephesians (3. 9–11): "On me ... he has bestowed this privilege ... of publishing to the world the plan of this mystery, kept hidden from the beginning of time in the all-creating mind of God. The principalities and powers of heaven are to see, now, made manifest in the Church, the subtlety of God's wisdom; such is his eternal purpose, centred in Christ Jesus our Lord."

And St Peter, in his first Epistle (1. 12): "The angels can satisfy their eager gaze", upon the message announced by the preachers of the Gospel through the Holy Ghost.

St Jerome, St Ambrose and the Greek Fathers interpret these passages simply as teaching that the angels had no knowledge whatever of the mysteries of salvation. A milder form, though still in my opinion exaggerated, of the view that the angels were kept in ignorance of the mystery of Redemption, is the belief that they only knew of it when, as they saw Christ ascending into heaven with the wounds of the Passion, and passing through their choirs they asked one another: "Who is this king of glory? Who is this, coming from Bosra, with garments deep-dyed?" These beautiful pictures have given rise to a whole literature since St Justin and have left their traces on the liturgy, but they are imaginary and make meaningless the whole teaching concerning the angels. They seem to me inconsistent with what is certain, especially the part played by the angels in the preparation for salvation, of which I shall speak. If they did not know the purpose of these preparations we must suppose that God entrusted them with their missions, as ministers but ill-informed of the purpose of their task. To imagine that they were kept in ignorance of the Mystery is to apply (whether consciously or not) to the order of Love harsh ideas of authority and obedience which are only too familiar to us.

St Augustine, St Gregory and all the western theologians thought, rather, that the angels had received in a general way the revelation of the divine decrees with regard to man's salvation, but not full, detailed knowledge of them (cf. Ia, Qu. 57, art. 9 ad 1; Qu. 117, art. 2 ad 1; IIa IIae, Qu. 2, art. 7 ad 1). The words of St Paul and of St Peter are sufficiently explained by the additional light which realization of God's plan gave them. St Peter's words, being intended to stir our feelings rather than provide knowledge, raise no difficulty. Those of St Paul are emphatic in the Semitic manner, and in the manner of an apostle, when obliged to minimize the work of the angels in the minds of his correspondents, who let themselves be carried away by extravagant speculations on the subject, and were in danger of giving the angels a worship due to Christ alone.

A second series of passages raises no difficulty, if they refer only to the wicked angels, but a sound exegesis does not interpret them so simply:

> [Christ] cancelled the deed which excluded us, the decree made to our prejudice, swept it out of the way, by nailing it to the cross; and the dominions and powers he robbed of their prey, put them to an open shame, led them away in triumph, through him. (Col. 2. 14–15.)

> [Christ] has taken his journey to heaven, with all the angels and powers and princedoms made subject under his feet. (1 Pet. 3. 22.)

> Full completion comes after that, when [Christ] places his kingship in the hands of God, his Father, having first dispossessed every other sort of rule, authority and power; his reign, as we know, must continue until he has put all his enemies under his feet. (1 Cor. 15. 24–5.)

These passages of course apply primarily to the devils. They can equally refer to human powers,[1] and also to Sin and Death personified: "in a word to all who oppose God's reign."[2] But there is something which should put us on our guard: the connection St Paul establishes between the commands of the Law and the angelic powers. We have seen from the first chapter that in the eyes of the Jews the Law had been given by angels. Not only does St Paul take this view into account, but he asserts such a close connection between Judaism and the angels, good and bad, that he includes the latter in the former's fall. In the view of St Stephen, as of the Jews, the mediation of the angels was for all those under the Law a title to glory, but to St Paul it is the sign of his imperfection (Gal. 3. 19–20).[3] The passages I have mentioned, while referring primarily to the wicked angels, in some sense declare that the work of all the angels is finished.[4] They are not responsible for the worship given them and, like the Law,

---

[1] O. Cullmann, *Dieu et César* (Appendix).
[2] Allo, *Première aux Corinthiens*, p. 408.
[3] Spicq, *L'Epître aux Hébreux*, t. II, p. 14.
[4] Daniélou, *Les anges et leur mission*, p. 20.

they are not bad in themselves. But just as to rely for salvation on the observance of the Law now that Christ has come
is to attach oneself to "the shadow of things to come", and to
live a slave to "the elements of the world" (Col. 2. 8, 18, 20),
so too to continue to pay worship to the angels is an
anachronism henceforth worthy of blame. The strong expressions of St Paul and of St Peter do not condemn the
good angels themselves, so far as they refer to them, but all
that men wrongly attribute to them, rank, power, rights,
which only belong to Christ. It is quite in the manner of
St Paul to dramatize this "robbery", to which Christ subjects
them. "We are speaking of a world that is to come; to whom
has God entrusted the ordering of that world? Not to angels"
(Hebr. 2. 5), as had been thought. The three passages I have
quoted are in the same spirit as that of Isaias (24. 21): "The
Lord will hold a reckoning with the hosts of heaven", when
he speaks of the stars made into gods by semitic paganism:
to "hold a reckoning" with them is to destroy them in the
spirit of the worshippers of these false gods.

The connection with the Law is very instructive. The
humiliation, the "destruction", of the heavenly powers is very
like the treatment given' by St Paul to the divine Law. He
treats it "as the great enemy of man, the supreme enemy
conquered by Christ".[5] Yet it is divine. Christ did not abrogate
it; he fulfilled it to the perfection of the Spirit (Mt. 5. 17). So,
too, the angels are refused the claims which had been made
for them and, in relation to Christ, play the subordinate part
proper to them. Because they had been mediators of the Law,
they are changed into its ministers, this being granted as a
divine privilege; they are regarded as masters of the whole
order governed by the Law, and thus are reduced to being
"spirits apt for service, whom he sends out when the destined
heirs of eternal salvation have need of them" (Hebr. 1. 14;

[5] Bouyer, *La Vie de saint Antoine*, p. 193. See especially Rom. 1–9
and Ephes. 2. 5.

cf. Apoc. 22. 6). There is no real degradation in this, and we must correct the description of them as having their work brought to an end. I shall only make use of the description to express, conditionally, the impression made by St Paul's teaching on the subject. Neither is the Law brought to an end; it too must henceforth play the part which comes back to it, of being at the service of the faithful to enlighten them concerning the conduct through which they will make incarnate the Spirit of Jesus. It becomes hateful if it is only a letter, not given life by his Spirit; then it inflicts death (2 Cor. 3. 6); it does mortal injury to whoever imagines it is enough, in the Christian order, to follow its commands, however holy they may be. Thus no angel has any right to the worship which belongs to God and to Christ. Every angel to which such worship was offered would cry at once, as in the Apocalypse (19. 10): "Never that; keep thy worship for God; I am only thy fellow servant, one of those brethren of thine who hold fast the truth concerning Jesus. It is the truth concerning Jesus that inspires all prophecy."

The phrase in the Epistle to the Hebrews ("spirits apt for service, whom he sends out when the destined heirs of eternal salvation have need of them") is certainly not exclusive. It can mean all those called to the kingdom of heaven, and hence all men[6]: "It is his [our Saviour's] will that all men should be saved, and be led to recognize the truth" (1 Tim. 2. 4). The ministry of the angels extends as far as the activity of Christ.

This ministry can only have the humble duty of preparation, because the union between Christ and those who enjoy his salvation must be direct. The Lord has shown this by the disappearance of angels in the Gospels, during the whole time that he personally manifested himself. We should take notice of this, for the events of the Gospel story are a practical teaching, which instructs us as much as our Lord's words

[6] Spicq, *op. cit.*, p. 57.

about the character of the world of grace. The angels openly carried out their duties before the coming of Christ and while he was a child. They helped him, too, in the desert, after the temptation. Then there is no further question of intervention on their part until the comfort they give on the night of the agony. After that Matthew (28. 2–4) describes the terrifying appearance of the angel of the Lord, who rolls away the stone from the tomb. This angel fills a double office of preparation: an external service done to Christ who raises himself from the tomb, and the announcement to the holy women (*ibid.*, 5–7). From this moment once again the angels often show their presence, indeed they play their part in a new work of preparation, that of the Church.

They had for long made preparations for the Incarnation: by their appearances, which all had in view the appearance of the Son of God in the flesh, an opinion accepted by St Thomas from St Augustine (Ia, Qu. 51, art. 2 ad 1; IIIa, Qu. 30, art. 3); by their ministry in giving the law; by the carrying out of God's interventions, whether for punishment or for help, which led forward the Chosen People, according to God's plan in preparation for the coming of the Saviour (Gen. 19. 13; Exod. 12. 23; 4 Kings 19. 35); by the help they gave to the prophets (3 Kings 19. 5–7; 4 Kings 1. 3 and 11; *ibid.* 6. 17); the part they played in the enlightenment of the latter by God (IIa IIae, Qu. 172, art. 2).

Their actions have been similar from the beginning of the Church, but they played no part in the actual resurrection of Christ, nor in the ascension, nor again in the descent of the Holy Ghost. But, just as long before their appearances foretold the coming of Christ, Christ made use of them to announce his resurrection, and directly after the ascension to announce his future return. They helped the apostles by setting them free (Acts 5. 19–20; 12. 7–11), and an angel struck the first ruler who persecuted the Church (Acts 12. 23). It was the action of an angel that caused the first extension of the Church beyond the Jewish world, the conversion of Cornelius the centurion (Acts 10. 3 and 55). It may be that in this incident it was providential that an angel should be mentioned as bringing about the pagan's approach to St Peter, while it was the direct action of the Spirit which inspired the head of the Church. It seems to me that in both cases the Spirit and the angels each worked in their different spheres, the former ruling over the whole action, the latter working through sensible effects, and the result could, of course, be attributed to either, as in the case of Philip the deacon (Acts 8. 26 and 39). In this case it can hardly also be by chance that the miraculous movement of Philip is attributed to the angel when Philip met the eunuch, and to the Spirit immediately after the coming of the Spirit in baptism.

Christ's work of salvation, in the ministry of which the angels play parts as varied as they are secret, must have that character of implacable warfare which our Lord and St Paul revealed to us in the first chapter, and which we must soon consider. In the eyes of our Lord it is not evil which exists, but the evil one (Matt. 6. 13; 13. 38). He is the prince of this world. If for St Paul our struggle has not been against flesh and blood, that is, against human enemies of whom we have direct experience, but against invisible enemies, against "those who have mastery of the world in these dark days, with malign influences in an order higher than ours" (Ephes. 6. 12), to enlightened spirits this is immediately evident. The whole purpose of their service is to give us strength in this warfare, as the whole purpose of Christ's redemption is to rescue us from the rule of Satan, and to take us into the Kingdom of his Love.

Thus they see our real wretchedness which comes from association with the devil, as is expressed in a collect in the Missal (17th Sunday after Pentecost). The many services they render us possess from this fact a character of mercy.

THE ANGELIC MINISTRY

St Bernard tells us of the three kinds of motive which influence them in this ministry. The passage seems emotional, but it is more profound than appears at first sight.

> The angels act for God, for us, and for themselves. For God: they reflect the great mercy with which he encompasses us: our likeness to them arouses their pity. Then for themselves: they eagerly desire to see us fill the places made empty in their ranks, for the lips of children, but lately fed with milk and not with solid food, ought to perfect the choir destined to celebrate the divine majesty. The angels have made a beginning, and in these firstfruits they already enjoy a wonderful happiness. But they wait for us with a great eagerness, and the desire to see this choir perfected urges them forward.
>
> (Sermon 1 for the feast of St Michael, n. 4.)

We gain a deep insight in this matter if we look at the action of the angels on our behalf as a movement which starts from God and returns to God, from his Providence which controls this action out of mercy, to the praise of God's glory, for which the angels should take us among them. From the beginning they are our friends with utmost intensity, that of the whole "weight of glory" which moves them, and into which they plunge.

Here on earth we shall not succeed in forming a satisfying idea of this ministry. We have only to remember the difficulty of understanding how spiritual influences can affect our conduct, actions and feelings. Being ourselves in part spirits, we can know something with certainty of the life of a spirit, whether of the angels, or with regard to God. But the intervention of spirits in what is involved in space and time and all that follows from this, is deeply mysterious. Even in our personal world, composed of spirit and body, we have no knowledge of the relationship between these two elements. Neurologists and psychologists, whatever advances they may make by experiment and analysis, only find out the manifestations which appear on the surface. The causality of psychic action on the body, and of the opposite process, escape our observation. With regard to the angels we cannot even make use of experiences enabling us to determine the circumstances in which they intervene, or the way in which they do so. We can never say that a particular good thought or fancy comes from them, or a particular movement of hope which gives us courage, or a particular presentiment which sets us on our guard. We do not know that particular phenomena produced in the world are to be attributed to them. The angels are ministers of one who is infinitely good, whose objects and methods remain infinitely mysterious; they hide their spiritual action under sense impressions or external facts, which we can explain sufficiently by ascertainable causes.

Our sources for knowledge of the nature of their ministry among us are Scripture and the witness of tradition, but only certain leading facts on the subject emerge. This has been made clear more than once. If now we wish to state more precisely how good angels behave in regard to man, we cannot judge how far the opinions belonging to particular epochs, circles or authors show supernatural authority. It is enough for our salvation that God and the Church tell us of the ministry of the angels, and enable us to have a general knowledge of the way it is carried out. Desire for further detail is apt to involve a curiosity which distracts us from what is essential. It may easily land us in a mass of uncertainties, and even of foolish theories, and may reduce to absurdity the important facts revealed by God, as well as the conclusions which can be truly deduced from them.

For example, angels undoubtedly preside over the meetings for Christian worship. But what does this mean? Since the liturgy of the Church is, on earth, a participation in that performed by the angels, it is a truism to say they are present at ours. What matters is that we should make ourselves present at theirs, and we do this if we carry out our worship with all our power. We should certainly believe that their ministry consists in the application of their praise to ours, so as to inspire it and carry it along in company with their spiritual effort. But it is hard to get beyond a rather crude picture of this, and to do justice to the Christian order, in which the movements of our hearts reach God without any intermediary, just as grace touches us directly.

With regard to this "presence" of the angels at our worship —and it is much more than merely ornamental—we have several sources of information, passages in the liturgy and a famous text from St Paul. The Apostle mentions their presence in order to urge Christians to behave themselves worthily. At that time when a veil for women was a sign of their position as virgins or married women, he told them to wear it "for the angels' sake" (1 Cor. 11. 10). Thus we see that the angels were looked upon as guardians and upholders of good order in the meetings for worship. Plainly it is important for us to revive in ourselves the attitude of deference to which they urge us.

But who is the "angel" mentioned by the Roman liturgy in the prayer of the Canon after the Consecration? The prayer begs God "to carry the offering through his angel to the altar on high". This prayer is nothing else, it appears, than the western equivalent of the epiclesis.[7] In this view an angelic minister is needed in the most profound and sublime part of the eucharistic sacrifice. We may, however, ask whether this "angel" is not a divine Person, the Word, as Fr de la Taille thinks.

What is meant by saying the angels "offer our prayers to

[7] Epiclesis is derived from two Greek words meaning "call" and "upon"—the Holy Spirit is called down upon the offerings. For a discussion of the question of the epiclesis in the Roman liturgy see F. Amiot. *History of the Mass*, pp. 102–3, in this series.

God" (Tob. 12. 12; Apoc. 5. 8; 8. 3–4)? The mystery of *intercession* is here in question. What greater power do our prayers gain, when they are taken up with the angelic praise, or into that of the saints? The fact cannot be doubted. The Church makes us say, for example, in the postcommunion of the feast of St Raphael (Oct. 24th): our prayers are of themselves of little worth, so may the archangel present them for God's blessing! Why? Plainly to give them additional merit: the charity which joins together the faithful in God, who is Love, has the power to make our prayers gain from the perfection of the angels and saints, when they make them their own. This is a wonderful example of that friendship with the angels to which this study should introduce us.

From the opposite point of view, the angels, says St John of the Cross, "do not only carry our prayers to God, but they also bring God's messages to our souls, feed them, as good fathers, with delightful inspirations and communications from God, and this they do by their spiritual mediation" (*Spiritual Canticle*).

Perhaps we now have a less inadequate idea of the way in which their influences act; they act, as I have said spirits act upon spirits, a thing of which we have some experience; they strengthen us, provide us with ideas and images, persuade us, and always for our salvation.

In order to describe more fully the angelic ministry in relation to other mediations, it is interesting to ask why the angels are not charged with the administration of the sacraments, ridiculous as such a question may appear at first sight. Nothing would prevent them having this power, if we only think of the sacraments as signs communicating grace to us (*Sent.* Bk. 4, dist. 5, Qu. 2, art. 3; *Summa Theol.* IIIa, Qu. 64, art. 7). But since these signs are sensible, the angels would have to appear to confer them, and they always hide themselves modestly behind their good acts. The sacraments must, too, be prepared and accompanied with a multitude of holy actions, rites, prayers and teachings which prepare the way for them, and which must have human qualities to dispose us to receive the grace profitably in view of the temporal, spatial, sensible, social, condition of our freedom. The angels, however, not being of our nature, cannot help to this extent with their mediation. Fundamentally, the sacramental order is that of the priesthood of Christ, in which they do not share. It is fitting that a mediator of the sacraments of human salvation should exercise this mediation in virtue of a personal experience of human nature. Christ is our high priest who can feel for us because he was not simply proved like the angels, but in our way, learning by his suffering obedience (Hebr. 5. 8). The angels certainly prepare us for the sacraments, but in a hidden and inward fashion.

It is an ancient and common belief of the Church, witnessed to by the rites and language of the liturgy, that they play this part of preparing us by means of every act of worship, from baptism, which makes us share in "the exaltation of Christ above the angelic worlds",[8] to extreme unction, which includes the following prayer begging for a kingly retinue for our entry into paradise: "At the moment when your soul leaves your body, may the bright company of the angels go before it, may the assembly of the apostles approach you to be your judge, may the triumphant army of martyrs clothed in white come to meet you, may the gleaming band of confessors surround you with lilies in their hands, may the exultant choir of virgins receive you, and may rest and happiness encompass you, in the bosom of the patriarchs."

[8] Daniélou, *Les anges et leur mission*, p. 83. Fr Daniélou gives in this work the opinions, often stimulating, of the Fathers (especially the Greek Fathers) about the activity of the angels in regard to us. It is impossible to summarize this evidence, in which imagination, sensibility, religious and popular traditions, clever speculations, have a very large part, and in which it is very difficult to decide what has a serious basis.

It is probable that the chief care felt by the angels in our service is for the right ordering of our minds, because they are spirit. "Their duty as guardians", says St Thomas (Ia, Qu. 113, art. 5, ad 2), "aims at enlightenment by teaching, as its ultimate and principal effect." Perhaps we may make the guess, with Dom Vonier who for his part asserts it as nothing else than the thought of St Thomas, "that the human race keeps its mental balance through the constant watchfulness of good spirits." In this respect modern times demand especial help.

I think that Jacques Maritain is deeply in touch with the true order of things when he writes:

> The philosopher is inconsolable for the irreparable loss of the least reality, however fugitive, that of an expression on a face, a movement of the hand, a free act, a musical harmony, wherever some love or beauty passes away. He has his explanation, I must admit, he believes nothing of all this passes away, because the angels keep all these things in their memory, and because, chosen freely by and in minds, they are in a better state there than in themselves; he believes the angels would never cease to tell these to one another, and to revive in them under countless forms the story of this poor earth. But do wise men trouble themselves with such problems?... It is through sympathy with the misery of creation that they do so.

THE SPIRITUAL WARFARE

What we know of the way in which pure spirits can act on one another gives us some idea of the warfare between the good and evil spirits. Spirits can only communicate their thoughts to one another, and try to persuade one another. It is useless for enemies such as these to try the latter method, because they are firmly fixed in glory or in evil. They can do nothing to change their wills.

Since all creatures are brothers, we can at least suppose that the choice made by the angels was not only a drama in which each of them and the creator took part, but that they urged one another forward, each trying to make the others follow his own choice. If their struggle began in this way before they were fixed in good or evil, it could not take on any other form than that of opposing efforts to persuade. Now that both sides have reached their decision, the warfare, being between pure spirits, can be only the expression of their contrary choices.

The picture of their warfare, however, as shown in the Apocalypse (12. 7 and 55), symbolizes that of the influence they exert on us. The wicked angels are stirred by a rage which causes such a hell as to exasperate them beyond measure; they can only escape from themselves by attacking others. They are cruel, because perverted. Since their sin was against God's love, and they are fixed in it, hatred of this Love and of all that it inspires is henceforth the principle governing their conduct.

Thus it is within these spirits that we must look for an explanation of their desire for strife. Any other view presents a psychology which is too childish to be probable in the case of these sublime spirits. A misleading picture was often drawn in antiquity, naturally in a variety of forms and, though such popular preaching was even put forward by holy doctors of the Church, we must not assign to it the authority of genuine tradition. According to this legend Lucifer was the angel appointed to govern our earth. When God created man, destined for personal union with him in the person of Christ, Lucifer was filled with envy, angry because he was not himself raised to this union. He revolted against God, caused man to fall, and henceforth tormented him. This picture is attractive, for it seems to explain the great facts given in the Bible concerning this drama, and also to explain the title "prince of this world", which is certainly that of the devil (John 12. 31; 14. 30; Ephes. 2. 2), and also the words of

Wisdom (2. 24), which say that "the devil's envy brought death into the world".[9] Many moderns, following Suarez, have revived some part of these ancient ideas, imagining that the devil's sin of pride was desire for the hypostatic union (St Thomas had already met this, Ia, Qu. 64, art. 1). All this bases the truths of faith on an arbitrary mythology, which leaves aside the essential motives.

In fact the action of the devils is the result, by a vital necessity, of their original choice, fixed for ever in perversion. It is far more effective than any other harm they can do that this is less deeply rooted in their being. In us it was only accidentally that it could succeed, for we are unassailable if we wish to be. Our spirit has all that it needs to protect itself, our will cannot be directly affected by any power, except that of God himself.

Unhappily the enemy finds a weak point in us, in the "malice" which through sin has altered our original tendency, and consequently in the dulling of our spiritual sense, the aberrations of our judgement, our repugnance to face difficulties (and our weakness soon causes everything to be hard), our proneness to follow inclinations which make us fall to the lowest depths.[10] Only Christ and the Blessed Virgin could say of the devil, "one is coming, who has power over the world, but no hold over me" (John 14. 30). The devil has no need to disclose himself, or to expose himself to special

[9] We have already seen that the title, "prince of this world", given to the devil, is sufficiently explained without such ideas. As to the passage in Wisdom it refers to the devil *after* his fall and when he tempted Adam. It seems indeed a witness to Jewish interpretations of the account in Genesis. If, however, this really gives us revealed teaching about the motive for the devil's temptation of man, we need look no further for an explanation of this "envy" than the attitude of a fallen being to one who was unfallen (full of anger because the pure spirit was higher by nature than man).

[10] I may refer here to the traditional doctrine of the four wounds left by original sin, aggravated by personal sin: "malice", "ignorance", "weakness" and "concupiscence".

attack. It is enough for him secretly to give more force to notions which of themselves pervert our will.

"He need only enter into the stream of our own inclinations, when we treat lightly things that lead us astray; he has only to press against that which already totters, to hold back that which seeks to rise. His influence spreads like a poisonous gas which we inhale without knowing it" (Sertillanges, *Catéch. des Incroyants* I, 186).

How many men attribute to the action of the devil follies they indulge in when their own inclinations are sufficient explanation. It is only too true that the powers of evil are at work in the elements of the external world and in man's passions, but they need not make any special efforts except against some saints who are not the playthings of "flesh and blood".

Some indications can be found in Scripture which show in what direction the instigations of the devils or the dispositions which, on our side, best favour them, are most serious. They act like the sparrows which eat God's seed when it does not fall upon "a noble and generous heart", but beside the path, so that it is trodden by the passions to which we give ourselves up (Luke 8. 12). They incite us to disobedience (Ephes. 2. 3), and we should understand this in the deep sense in which we have seen that they disobeyed, though obviously this is manifested in acts of disobedience in the usual sense. They rouse in us the natural appetites of the flesh (*ibid*. 3), because we are especially vulnerable here, and also undoubtedly because the perversity of a pure spirit may probably direct its sadism towards a frantic scorn of sensuality. The parable of the strong man armed (Luke 11. 21–8) teaches us to redouble the efforts we should make, when the devils have not succeeded in their temptations.[11]

[11] On the danger of temptations from the devil: 1 Cor. 7. 5; 2 Cor. 2. 11; 4. 4; 11. 3, 14; Ephes. 4. 27; 6. 11–12; 1 Thess. 3. 5; 2 Thess. 2. 9; 1 Tim. 3. 7; 5. 15; 2 Tim. 2. 26.

These powerful intelligences, clever, inventive and acute as they are, can do nothing against a simple heart. It has its foundation in faith, in the full sense given by the New Testament to this word. It is nothing else than faith which resists the devil (1 Peter 5. 9; 1 John 5. 4–5; 1 Tim. 6. 12), faith as answering the unfailing faithfulness of God, and finding all its strength in union by love with Christ the conqueror: "Who will separate us from the love of Christ . . . no angels or principalities or powers" (Rom. 8. 35, 38). "We are conquerors through him who has granted us his love" (*ibid*. 37).

Now, is it not remarkable that, in the matter of this warfare, the New Testament does not urge us to turn towards the good angels to overcome the bad? Faith in God, faith in Christ, love of Christ, recourse to the weapons of God "to draw your strength from the Lord" (Ephes. 6. 10–17; cf. Rom. 13. 12; 1 Thess. 5. 6), being assured that God "will not allow you to be tempted beyond your powers" (1 Cor. 10. 13), prayer for this and for deliverance from the evil one (Matt. 6. 13)—of all this we are assured, and there is no question of angels. "There is a stronger power at work in you, than in the world" (1 John 4. 4).

Yet we are told that in fact countless angels assist us, suggesting to us thoughts contrary to those which the devils suggest, substituting their persuasion for those of these tempters, strengthening us, and baffling their ingenuity. While the rebel spirits depend only on themselves, the good angels are so wholly servants that all they do in the warfare depends on their Head. We have the advantage of this when we are united to him. Their help is not made plain to us on earth. Here we celebrate their feast, but it is in heaven that we shall see how their "patronage" has helped us.[12]

---

[12] Collect for the feast of St Gabriel, March 24th: *Ut qui festum ejus celebramus in terris, ipsius patrocinium sentiamus in coelis*—"as we celebrate his feast on earth, so we may feel the strength of his protection in heaven".

THE GUARDIAN ANGEL

One angel clearly deserves a special interest on our part, since he is specially appointed to us: our "guardian angel". It is a belief so common in the Church that we ought to call it "of faith" that angels are appointed by God to watch over and help human beings. All the catechisms teach it (*Catechism of the Council of Trent*, 4, 9, n. 4). It seemed assumed by our Lord, when in connection with children he mentions their "angels". (Matt. 18. 10.) From the earliest days of Christianity this belief was so taken for granted that the faithful gathered at the house of Mary, mother of John Mark, thought it natural that the angel of the imprisoned apostle Peter should come to visit them (Acts 12. 15). Nowadays most of the faithful hardly think of these guardians, when speaking of angels. This is to be regretted for two reasons: our spirit and our heart should, as I have urged throughout, open out to the whole world of angels and, secondly, devotion to our guardian angel is often as purely utilitarian as trust in St Antony of Padua for finding things we have lost. Yet who knows if ideas and ways of acting which are too material may not involve a spiritual sense higher than appears?

However this may be, we ought to understand, following St Thomas (Ia, Qu. 113, art. 1), the meaning and importance of belief in the guardian angels. It is in an order still more fundamental than that of redemptive grace—in the order of God's government of all creatures. The Creator does not abandon creatures when he has made them exist; he sees that they shall have what they need for natural perfection. Man is too unstable if left to himself; under the pressure of his inclinations he is in too great danger of error when he judges what he should do. Hence God provides him with a rule to tell him what is right and, since he is a living being, a rule so living that it is a personal being. The rule of law is too abstract. In his imagination, amid passions, which are in danger of surprising him, God, by means of an angel, intro-duces images and tendencies leading him to do what is right. It is often necessary that there should be suggested to him the concrete forms which the good he ought to do assumes in different cases, and for him in the precise circumstances of his life and personal character. Nothing more is suggested than impressions, insights, suggestions, in no way forcing men's liberty, and once the good counsel is given, leaving them "to the arbitrament of their own wills" (Ecclus. 15. 14).

Baudelaire, Péguy and Claudel had a lively appreciation of what the assistance of our guardian angel can do. The rebel he must rebuke vigorously, he is wonderfully cunning with the ambitious man, the poet and the man of prayer he inspires like music.

Péguy writes to Joseph Lotte: "I have an amazing guardian angel: he is more cunning than myself! I am protected, and cannot escape him. Three times I have felt him seize me, and snatch me from what I wanted to do, from acts I had planned and determined. His tricks are incredible!"

Claudel writes:

If our heart is base we sadden the angel, and give him no more reward than a piece of dry wood or insensible matter. But once the pilgrim and his companion have begun to con-verse, who can stop him! What happiness it is to listen to him, and how much we have to tell him! Then we learn how, as the Apocalypse says (21. 17), "the measure of an angel is that of a man."[13] The conduct which makes us progress is both ours and his. By ourselves we are not capable of that nobility, and at the same time of that modesty and confidence. The tune which from time to time I recall to encourage myself, like the song I used to teach my children, I learnt from him.... He has made me see everything in a fresh light.... In everything he causes

[13] The words quoted do not refer to a general law, as Paul Claudel seems to think. It is *this* angel who, in St John's vision, uses for his measuring the usual measure of a man.

my right actions and the good I do, and makes all around me harmonious, ideal, reasonable and praise of God.

(*Présence et prophétie*, pp. 249–50.)

The idea of the guardian angel which these passages illustrate, and give in an extreme form, is fully consistent with all Christian thought. When such an idea is developed more precisely in the tradition of classical Greek philosophy, it sees in the guardian angel the best example of what it takes for a general principle: "that which is subject to movement and change is moved and determined by that which is without movement or change" (Ia, Qu. 113, art. 1). The guardian angel does not seem to St Thomas to be required only on account of the danger of failure and to ensure a nobler life; he thinks that principles "which do not move or change" should be directly present to that which changes. In the concrete order these principles are spirits. St Thomas thus sees the guardian angel as resulting from the world order, as I must presently explain.

Whatever school of philosophy we may follow, an understanding of the work of the guardian angel, as I think it should be understood, that is, in its place in the whole order of creation, implies that every man has the benefit of his aid, not only the faithful, and has it from the first moment of independent life, from birth (Ia, Qu. 114, art. 5). Clement of Alexandria, Tertullian and Origen thought that only Christians had guardian angels, and that they received them at baptism.[14] Christ alone on earth did not have one, his Person itself being the supreme rule of all rightness: the

---

[14] It is certainly not necessary to refer to this ancient belief in order to explain today that prayer used in the preparatory ceremony at baptism of adults, which, nevertheless, probably originated in this belief: "O God, who hast brought the children of Israel out of the land of Egypt, sending the angel of your goodness to guard them day and night, grant, we beseech thee, that thou mayst send from heaven thy holy angel, who may guard thy servant now present, and lead him to the grace of baptism."

divine Word (Qu. 113, art. 4). The worst sinners have this faithful and kindly friend, who arranges meetings, and inspires dispositions able to bring them back to the right path.

The help of the angel is unfailing. It is not confined to passing services, which are carried out by the angels in special circumstances. The common belief is that everyone has his own. An angel is intelligent enough to concern himself with several people at once but, as he devotes himself entirely to the act of applying his "power" to someone, he cannot at the same time do so to another, and this consecration of an angel to each human being is in harmony with the personal character of vocations, with the inestimable value of each soul; it is precisely in connection with this value that our Lord alludes to the angel guardians.

We may suppose that men charged with great responsibilities receive a second angel to guard them in the duties they perform in the service of nations, since these duties are of such a different kind from their personal destiny. This angel is, without doubt, that of the nation; it is right that it should be he who assists the head of the state (*Sent*. Bk. 2, dist. 11, art. 2, ad 4). St Thomas fancied that he should be an archangel, or one of the "principalities" (Qu. 113, art. 3).

A human community has great need of an angel. It has a collective consciousness, a mentality, it is subject to the impulse of passions. Daniel (10. 13) speaks of him "who guards the realm of Persia". The difficulty about this passage is that Michael and this angel "fight", while the latter does not seem to be a devil. We can avoid this difficulty quite easily, for these words of Daniel represent an opinion of the prophet's time in accordance with which the prophet framed his teaching; it is not itself his teaching. We can also see here a symbolizing, through imaginary angels, of the rivalries among nations. But this "warfare" between the angels of hostile nations may very well be, as St Thomas thought (*Sent*. Bk. 2, dist. 11, Qu. 2, art. 5), the opposition between different merits of these nations, which these angels plead before God, not even they themselves being able to see how they can be reconciled deep in the divine judgement. As to the "angels of the churches", at the beginning of the Apocalypse, Fr Bernard Allo remarks (*L'Apocalypse*, p. 48): "While agreeing that they are personifications of the community rather than angelic or human persons, the name which signifies them implies the existence, and then the symbolical notion, of guardian angels." St Gregory Nazianzen, when leaving his beloved Church of Constantinople, greeted the angel, begging him to see "that there be no hindrance to bar its people on their way to the heavenly Jerusalem". The most interesting feature of this teaching, that human communities are assisted by angels who look after their spiritual interests even so far as to appear to "struggle" with one another, is, as Fr Daniélou (*op. cit.*, p. 28) explains, that it encourages missionary effort. The messengers of the Gospel have in them supporters, who prepare the ways to Christ, even before the arrival of the Good News, giving a worth to what is true in the thought of these people and to what is good in their customs.

Of course, since the whole created order is in subjection to Christ, the guardian angel directs towards this King of the universe the person or community committed to him. It goes without saying that for this purpose he must fight against the influence of devils upon his ward. We may ask whether the latter is subject only to occasional attacks or whether a wicked angel is also attached to him to try him, the good angel taking care that the trial should not be too great. The idea at once repels us. Yet, who can tell? Our instinctive feeling in this matter may perhaps fail to see the true depths. We are sure of the existence of the guardian angel, who makes concrete for each of us the principle of right, and we are sure that we are tempted through the suggestions of devils. There is no reason why these suggestions should not be applied, throughout our lives, to our personal tendencies by a single devil who knows us well. This way of looking at the thing makes concrete the idea of the "two ways", so strongly emphasized in early Christianity (from the time of the *Didache*, which dates between 50 and 70), an idea which should be fundamental for every Christian. The doctrine of the two angels is not of faith, but it is authorized by ancient tradition (not spelt with a capital T). We find it already in the Pastor of Hermas, in Origen, St Athanasius, St Gregory of Nyssa, and it is still familiar to St Vincent de Paul. I will only quote the passage from Hermas:

> A man has two angels: an angel of justice, and an angel of evil. The angel of justice is tender, reserved, sweet and peaceful. When he comes to your heart he speaks at once to you of justice, holiness, temperance and every right work. When these thoughts rise in your heart, know that the angel of justice is with you. The angel of evil, on the other hand, is quick to anger, full of bitterness and madness. Know him by his works. [This further passage should be added:] Do not fear the devil. . . . He can only frighten you, but it is an empty fear: do not fear him, and he will flee away from you. . . . He cannot rule over the servants of God, who put all their hope in God. He can fight, but not conquer. So, if you resist him, he will flee away from you.

Having spoken in general of the activity of the good angels on our behalf, I need not say more about the activity of the guardian angels; it is like that of the others, but made to suit our individual needs with the insight of a friend. Without doubt they render the most humble services to their wards. If we ask their help in some small matter, such as waking up earlier than usual, getting a place in a crowded train, being warned in advance of something we need to know, the ready help we receive shows clearly their intervention. But a real good must be in question, never a reply to vain curiosity about the invisible world. A prayer to the angel guardians often proposed by pious authors is to keep guard over the bodily senses. In ancient times they were often compared to shepherds or to teachers.

The most characteristic things the Fathers say about the guardian angel may be summed up under three heads: purification, penitence and prayer; purification, to assure peace of the soul: he is "the angel of peace"; penitence: this idea is to be found throughout the Pastor of Hermas—the angel presides over the penitence of his ward, so that, in the words of Clement of Alexandria, "he shall have nothing more to repent of when he leaves the body, nor to be ashamed of when he sees the Lord coming with his army". Plainly the angel guardian "offers up the prayers" of his ward, for he always sees the face of the Father; "he prays with us," says Origen, "and works with us".

He tells the soul, as St Bernard says, "Set your pleasure in the Lord, and he shall hear you", "Attend to the Lord, and keep his ways". "If he delays, ever be on the watch, for he will surely come soon"; he shows the soul to the Lord: "O God, my whole soul longs for thee, as a deer for running water."

The liturgy of the sick directs us to ask their guardian angels "to guard, comfort, protect, visit and defend them." The well-known prayer to the guardian angel, composed in the seventeenth century, is a summary of the opening words of the long poem of an English monk at the end of the eleventh century.[15] It runs as follows: "Angel of God, my guardian, guard me today, enlighten me, rule and govern me, for I have been entrusted to you by God's goodness."

Newman finishes the Dream of Gerontius (January, 1865) with these words spoken by the angel to the soul he has guarded, and which has not been sufficiently obedient to him to merit the vision of God immediately after death, a vision which one who is not wholly purified cannot sustain:

[15] The lines are published, with other ancient prayers to the angel guardians, by Dom Wilmart, *Auteurs spirituels et textes dévots* (p. 554).

Softly and gently, dearly ransomed soul
In my most loving arms I now enfold thee,
And, o'er the penal waters, as they roll,
  I poise thee, and I lower thee, and hold thee.
And carefully I dip thee in the lake,
  And then, without a sob or a resistance,
Dost through the flood thy rapid passage take,
  Sinking deep, deeper, into the dim distance.
Angels, to whom the willing task is given
  Shall tend, and nurse, and lull thee, as thou liest;
And Masses on the earth, and prayers in heaven,
  Shall aid thee at the throne of the Most Highest.
Farewell, but not for ever! brother dear,
  Be brave and patient on thy bed of sorrow,
Swiftly shall pass thy night of trial here,
  And I will come and wake thee on the morrow.

CHAPTER V

THEIR PART IN THE
WORLD ORDER

Historians of doctrine are very fortunate. Their business is to set down what men have thought in former times, but as to deciding what is true among all these opinions, they leave us to find out for ourselves. We have now arrived at this point and our task is difficult indeed. Are pure spirits set to perform special duties in the material order?

It is not certain that Scripture teaches this as revealed by God, nor does the Church tell us anything. Traditions, which through the centuries have asserted this doctrine, important as they are, can only be human, and it is impossible for us to decide whether they are the product of Tradition. What, then, is the value of our opinions, which can prove nothing for certain about this? They are rather the expression of probabilities which seem to harmonize with the certain facts.

We are tempted to get rid of the problem by saying it is unimportant. We have enough to do in grasping the realities certainly revealed in the message from above. Since this does not plainly tell us of a part in the world-order assigned to the angels, knowledge of such a part cannot be necessary for salvation. This is true, and from the first pages of this book the reader will have realized that we must put the right values upon things in the supernatural order. It is one of the worst

ways of debasing the faith—unfortunately, only too frequently
done—to trouble ourselves with secondary matters not supernaturally guaranteed, while not accepting what is essential
with the firmness and interest it requires. We have seen how
abruptly St Paul cut short fanciful speculations about the
angels.

But the contemplative soul, or the mind anxious to view
the universe in the clear light of the faith, finds puzzling
words in Scripture which seem to assert a ministry of the
angels in regard to the elements of the world, and traditions,
also puzzling, which point in the same direction. They make
a striking impression on one who examines the world in a
religious spirit. If we keep clearly in mind the different kinds
of assent we should give to beliefs, if we remember what is
only conjecture, it is of value for our faith, while starting
from the greater realities, to branch out into the lesser ones,
or those less certain.

To the seer of Patmos angels usually control fire (Apoc. 14.
18), water (16. 5) and, sometimes at least, wind (7. 1). But the
inspired teaching that he proffers does not turn on these
visions; he means us to elucidate it from each scene viewed
as a whole and from certain features which are plainly important; the pictures themselves are derived from conceptions
belonging to his historic background. So, too, when our Lord
speaks of the Last Judgement, the disturbance of the "powers
of heaven" (Matt. 24. 29) is only intended to be one picture
among others to show us that the present world will end, and
that this will be terrible: that is his teaching, not a revelation
of angelic powers which will make the heavens rock. Such a
revelation would be very surprising, if we bear in mind the
imagery of the prophetic apocalypses (Isaias 13. 10; 24. 4;
Ezech. 32. 8; Joel 2. 10; 4. 15, etc.) where there is no question
of angels. When Psalm 148 invites all the elements to praise
God, when it sees them "execute God's decree", this implies,
in the historic context in which this psalm was sung, the idea

that these elements were given life by the angels; such an idea was universal in Judaism. Yet this does not oblige us to see in the "storm-wind" a pure spirit. St Paul may perhaps have been personally influenced by these ideas, without ever having had to ask himself seriously what was their value (cf. Gal. 3. 19; 4. 3; Col. 2. 15, 18). Or has divine inspiration guaranteed them through him? The Church on earth has thrown no light on the question, and we must remain uncertain—no doubt the Church has more urgent tasks.

Moreover St Paul and St John are noticeably restrained in this matter. The non-canonical Jewish literature, on the other hand, delighted in the fullest and most detailed assertions, implying this kind of animism. It may be said that this did not affect the Old Testament itself; it was the rabbis who interpreted Genesis, the prophets and the psalms in this way. We should notice it was animism of a special kind, carefully distinguishing the spirits from the elements over which they were set, and from God, whose ministers they were. Yet if we look at the matter as a natural phenomenon, it was an un-scientific animism, such as we laugh at today, and such as any doctrine concerning the place of the angels in the world order must entirely renounce. Later Judaism taught the names of the angels of the elements, and gave them duties in detail. For example, Cazardia had to see that the sun rose every day at the right time, and set at the right time. Each hour of the day had its angel.[1]

As the Fathers lived in a hellenized world, full of genii, and as, when they sought to understand the Old Testament, they were in some degree dependent on Judaism, they adopted this mentality as naturally as they spoke their own language. St Jerome was an exception. He opposed it, saying that a dispensation of Providence was enough to explain the order

---

[1] For amusement, the astonishing chapter in Chateaubriand's *Génie du Christianisme*, which takes this line, though following the worst form of "poetical" rhetoric, should be consulted; it is fantastically funny.

of things: there was no need for Holy Scripture to be cor-
rupted by Pseudo-Enoch (*On Habacuc*, I, 14). But Origen,
Ambrose or Augustine could think, as the last of these says,
that "every visible thing in this world is put under the charge
of an angel" (*Book on the Eighty-Three Questions*).[2] He did
not hesitate to write: "The angels manage natural things, as
the natural order requires, according to the will of him to
whom all is subject" (*De Genesi ad litteram* VIII, 24, 45).
Thus natural things are not sufficient for what their order
requires! Such a view was neither illogical nor foolish for
St Augustine. It was deeply thought out, and flowed from his
conviction of a danger of failure, inherent in created natures.
This notion was religious and emphasized personality to the
point of supposing a multitude of personal providences by
which was exercised the Providence of the heavenly Father.
These saw that everything should work together for the glory
of God, and the salvation of the elect. This view is so
essentially Christian and so in keeping with the whole supernatural order, that we cannot help asking if in some form it
is not necessary—provided it does not degenerate into un-
scientific animism.

With this tendency another is often combined, but this
other is inspired by a totally different spirit. It has received
from Aristotle and Averroës its most complete form. According to this theory the universe, far from leaving scope for
freedom, is, in the strictest sense, a *cosmos*: a system organized
so exactly that its order is necessary. It is closed in space,
made of incorruptible spheres of which the earth is the centre,
and in it the stars are fixed and revolve regularly. It is cyclic
in time, subject to the unalterable law of endless return; it
has not been created, and will last for ever. The pure intelligences make this machinery work, seeing that it obeys
necessity. The last among these intelligences is shared in

[2] *De diversis questionibus octoginta tribus*, to be found in Migne,
Patrologia Latina, 40, 116.

common by all men. Nothing could be more opposed than
this to the spirit of the Bible. Such is the cosmology which
ancient philosophy bequeathed through the Arabs to minds
which tried to picture to themselves the universe, the cosmology which gained their adherence as scientific! The genius
of St Thomas developed it in every way required by the faith,
but he adopted the combination of heavenly spheres moved
by minds, and in these he recognized angels. The various
species, fixed for ever in this regular world, also seemed to
him to demand pure spirits to control them. The part played
by the angels in the world order, if there is such a part, is
open to the suspicion of having been thought of in connection
with a system which has been completely discredited.

The clear-sighted poetic genius of Dante did not save him.
In the Divine Comedy a whole choir, not a single intelligence,
moves each sphere. Round that point which is God, a point
of fire so brilliant that no sight can endure it, turns a circle of
fire, moving with incredible rapidity and measured by the
strong love which inflames it: it is the circle of Seraphim.
The other choirs surround it, going less and less quickly, and
each circle makes one of the heavenly spheres revolve. This
is a strange scheme. More difficult than to represent it
spatially is to imagine the psychology of these acts of freedom and love which, having no choice about their effects,
only produce necessity. It is a strange philosophy of obedience!
It is necessary, in order that love may move "the sun and the
stars", that it should change these wonderful intelligences,
these beings with their sovereign freedom, and keen love, into
a kind of rocking horse. Dante declares without a smile that,
immediately after the fall of the devils, that part of the angels
which remained faithful "began this movement which you
behold with such pleasure that it has never ceased to revolve"
(*Paradiso*, Canto 29, verse 52; cf. Canto 28, vv. 16, 25–45,
89–96). Now we no longer make them turn the spheres, are we
going to find them work to do in the disappearing galaxies?

Whether we conceive the activity of the angels in the universe in the first or second way, there is an idea which comes naturally to the mind. We have met it already in reference to the spiritual warfare, and now we must consider it for a moment. There must have been a large number of angels in charge of the elements, who fell with their prince, the "prince of this world". They must make use of their power over the world to trouble it. These are "those who have mastery of the world in these dark days", dark through their evil doing, "with malign influences in an order higher than ours" (Ephes. 6. 12). Does not this theory explain the evil which troubles us, even in the physical world? Does it not account for "the whole of nature" groaning "in a common travail"?

As I have said, this notion is common in the Fathers. It does not appear to be scriptural, though some masters of exegesis have accepted it. It is unsatisfactory because it is really a useless subterfuge, trying to clear God of blame for nature's cruelty. Here I need not deal with the grave problem of the evil present throughout creation.[3] Deep thought is needed to meet this problem: first, we must state it correctly, not looking at the pain in creation, especially among the animals who prey on one another, as though they had human feelings, and, secondly, we must grasp how inevitable these evils are when there live together beings so diverse, complex and passing. It does not seem necessary to look for an explanation in the malice of wicked angels, and the theory is very like that which sees in these evils an effect of the sin of Adam. After this sin, it says, the lions, who had previously fed on vegetables, became carnivorous. In spite of the undoubtedly profound feeling which produces this theory, St Thomas judged it entirely unreasonable. I think it implies before man's creation an incredible disturbance, if we explain

[3] See *The Problem of Evil* in this series.

the evil in the world by the wickedness of fallen angels who were rulers of this world.

"No part of Scripture—certainly not St Paul—plainly asserts a disturbance of the general order of the world through the devils, while here and there we have mention of temptation from the devil.[4]. . . . The Gospel never shows us in the natural world around us anything else than the action of a fatherly Providence, though it reminds us of its small value and passing character. . . . On the other hand the evil one is only mentioned in passages where man is concerned. . . . Man is set in a world which, from the first, was in harmony with his dangerous state at a time of testing, and which will one day be in harmony with his glorification."[5]

Personally I cannot agree with the theory I have described and, without it, I have given a sufficient explanation of the puzzling expressions of St Paul. One of the strongest objections to this over-simple theory is to misrepresent St Paul's use of "world", "elements", "law" and all the old order, which are by no means bad in themselves, and only imply something wrong, if we confine ourselves to them, while they work for our salvation in the new order, in the world finally perfected in Christ risen and glorified. The angels, I repeat, are closely bound up with this world, "emptied" with him if we put them before Christ in any fashion, but really ministers of the restoration of all things in this new order, in Christ triumphant. It is a serious matter to upset this view of the completely ambivalent nature of the world by imagining an evil influence affecting its essential structure, and even explaining thereby the existence of physical evil—which is in fact inevitable in this contingent and complex world.

Nevertheless, it is certain that the wicked angels do every

[4] 1 Cor. 7. 5; 2 Cor. 11. 3, 14; Ephes. 2. 2; 6. 11–12; 1 Thess. 3. 5; 1 Peter 5. 8; James 4. 7, etc.

[5] A. M. Dubarle, "Le gémissement des créatures", in *Revue des Sciences Philosophiques et Théologiques*, 1954, pp. 451, 463–4.

kind of harm to it. One form of the "warfare" which the good
angels wage against the wicked is without doubt the preven-
tion or putting right of their evil deeds. The devils certainly
have power over places, objects and persons, as the exorcisms
show. The good angels thus have on occasion much to do in
the world order.

I think, however, they must have a regular office to perform.
In my opinion, we must say this, if we take seriously the idea
of spirit as revealed to us.

I must explain. There is no question of introducing into the
forces studied by modern physics, and which it has discovered,
on their own level, influences of spiritual origin, which would
be supposed to unite with these forces to produce phenomena.
I do not think angelic influence could ever be established to
exist as such, in the way that physicists have discovered pro-
tons, cosmic rays or radar. We shall not examine the world to
find a place for spiritual action of this kind, and it is surprising to see admirable writers devoting many pages to its
denial. Two assertions are enough, appealing to the exactness
which is the glory of modern science: the explanation of the
facts, in the sphere of science, should be given on the level of
this data; in this sphere we should consider as scientifically
non-existent "that which the mind cannot experience in the
data".

It is just conceivable that we should not exclude the possibility of pure spirits acting in the complex of elements, when
undoubtedly there is scope for indetermination. But this
theory is difficult: indetermination may well only be relative
to our insufficient knowledge of the elements in question (we
should remember how science progresses before committing
ourselves). It is not from a study of those elements which are
the subject of modern physics that we shall be able to
understand any action that pure spirits may perform in the
world.

Of course, an immense field is open to this action wherever

man intervenes. A simple example may be given which I have already mentioned in passing. The many, varied and striking occasions on which events prayed for occur make us think that, for instance, it is due to the kind action of an angel that the carriage of a train draws up just by one of their friends, who is standing on a crowded platform. If this is so, how are we to explain it? Do they act upon the engine? More likely they act among the images and other psychic events which cause their friend to stand, for no reason he is aware of, exactly on that spot and not a foot farther on—or perhaps they act upon the driver of the train.

Obviously the field thus open is immense. We must add also the field of truly human actions when a man makes a choice, for angels can enlighten and strengthen the mind and persuade the will. We must remember that free will can accept or refuse what they suggest, even though a man has no doubt that it comes from them. Their influence is exerted amid the innumerable elements out of which finally emerges the will's decision. When souls of good will reflect and act, the impressions which the angels stir up in them can often be the determining factor, and very probably a multitude of angels are always at work to direct men's actions according to God's plan. Thus the whole field of human affairs, and of man's activities in the world is the object of their care.

We must not exclude the possibility of direct action on the part of the angels upon matter, though we have no idea how it takes place. Granting certain facts, we must agree that they do this, as, for instance, at the time of the resurrection, when they rolled back the stone from the tomb (Matt. 28. 2), or at the deliverance of St Peter (Acts 12. 7–11), or in similar events in the lives of the saints. We must not say the angels do not act upon the engine of the train, though how they do so is very difficult. Here we have the main thing which, from the scientific point of view, is unscientific. Fr A. M. Dubarle (in the article I have referred to), however, justly remarks that, if reasons of theology and facts oblige us to assert the power of superhuman spirits on material things, "we can hardly deny this on scientific or philosophical grounds", since, "we do not know precisely by positive science how our own human spirit acts on the body, in order through it to affect the surrounding world". This must be admitted, but how we should like to be able to know something about it! Claudel surprises us, when he says: "If we wish to understand the connection between a spiritual rhythm and physical movement, we need only think of a dance, and reflect how the music passes from the composer's brain to the instruments of the players, and to the legs of the dancers" (*Présence et Prophétie*, p. 277).

The poet is not at a loss for comparisons, but it must be admitted that comparisons are not arguments:

> I fancy that creatures in different orders of being are in a "metaphorical" relationship with one another, so that each is aware of the influence of the other, as an orchestra follows the first violin. I may also compare this activity to a phenomenon of electricity, in which differing currents react differently, by comparison rather than by contact—or again that physical phenomenon, called catalysis, when an element, of itself inert, determines merely by its presence the interaction of two elements which otherwise do not affect one another. . . .
>
> The action of the angels on material things is exercised by influence rather than by direct causality, by spiritual rather than by physical activity, by an effect which is not material, by resonance. It is the influence of a note over its harmonic complement.   (*Ibid.*, p. 230–1.)

We must simply admit the incapacity of our minds on this subject.

The occasional interventions of angels are not on the deepest level. We may perhaps suppose that they have a normal, and constant, duty (Claudel had this in mind in his final sentences) in regard to the cosmic elements. Until now we have inquired what activity of the angels could affect the world in a way which modern science examines. Obviously it could not recognize these theories as scientific, because not only can it never establish angelic activity by its methods, but the question can never arise for it. It can never form a hypothesis on this subject but until now we have been looking at its universe, which is that of phenomena (the opening of Christ's tomb comes under this heading).

Now this is to take too narrow a view, and to have too timid a belief in spirit. We are quite right in finding a place for what, in the plan of phenomena, shows signs of an external spiritual cause.

Really to believe in spirit involves belief in its constant power in the universe, even in the midst of matter. Even in material things there must be a controlling idea of what they are and of what they do, what the scholastics call their "form". It is at a deeper level in them than the properties which can be sensed and measured and cannot, therefore, be a subject for modern science. It is the impression in a being of the creative idea which God has of this being. It is the ultimate source of the idea which we ourselves frame of that being, though usually we only tend towards it, and in most cases must be content with determining the phenomena.

Really to believe in spirit, with supernatural faith, is to deny that the vast machine of this world in which our immortal destinies are decided is outside the control of the Providence of the divine Spirit, which is anxious to make the elements play their part in bringing these destinies to their true end. The natural order itself must be penetrated with supernatural activity.

We must believe in spirit: it is not impersonal, a vague, indistinct element. It is personal—multipersonal. It does not exist only in the Father, the Word and the Holy Ghost, and in human beings. It also exists in the countless angels, in a higher degree than in us. The question of the power of spirit in the universe is thus in practice that of the works in the universe which concern the divine Persons, the angels and ourselves.

The work of the angels we shall be able to understand, if we bear in mind what the faith teaches us about God's government and the purpose of this universe. In short it is this:

God governs beings by means of one another. He does not only grant them being, and he does not treat them as mere instruments for his action: he gives them a certain independence from the beginning, and their own activity, in conformity with what they are, and which belongs to them individually. Plainly, then, the angels have a part to play in the universe, in its structure and in its working. This must correspond with the motive of their intelligence which, instead of depending for its operation on things, has a determining effect on things.

It is for the sake of spirits that the material universe exists. Pure spirits, however, do not need it, and that leaves incarnate spirits. We have need of the physical world to maintain and develop all that concerns our bodies—and hence the indefinite advance of material civilization—and our minds, in their state of union with our bodies, make no advance in knowledge, do not open out to any reality whatever, and are not perfected, except in connection with sensible things. We do not build up ourselves unless we build something in the world; we do not grow in love unless we consume ourselves in a service which puts us in touch with matter, even our most spiritual knowledge is a reading of signs made to us by the world.

Undoubtedly this world only appears to our natural experience and to modern science as an inextricable play of energies which produce their effects blindly and of necessity. When certain minds, as for example, Fr Teilhard de Chardin, see in it a spiritual purpose, they are abused and accused of inventing unfounded theories. The least we can say of this world is that its meaning is extremely puzzling to the mind which only has its natural light. We need that the eyes of our heart should be enlightened in order to recognize its meaning. Then our eyes see its meaning, which is to become, by the use we make of it, in conformity with the will of its, and our, Creator, praise to his glory. It is, we realize, for us to give it this meaning, but it is not left to our fancy to settle this. A "controlling idea of what beings are, an impression in them of the creative idea of God" guides us, but with a certain obscurity. As to its origin, it certainly comes directly from God. Yet God, in conformity with the great law of his government, arranges for the help of his angels in freeing it from matter, and for the perfection of beings according to this idea. St Thomas compares the angels to husbandmen who, in the field of creation, help beings to grow (de Veritate, Qu. 5, art. 8 ad 4). He attributes to angelic thought, reflecting God's thought of beings, the high degree of intelligibility which they possess. By their action in our souls, and by the deep tendency they give to beings, the angels cause our destinies and the universe to correspond. It is through them that the universe tends to be a cosmos, a coherent and complete organization; it will only be this in perfection in the new heaven and the new earth. The angels are secretly preparing this earth and these heavens in the visible world, which we cannot truly think of now, as the Greeks did, as a real cosmos, except by an optimistic judgement, based only on hope, of what it may become. Without faith, faith in the work of the angels, there is danger of this belief being unfounded. With it we see the world having a part in our supernatural re-creation, as it had in our creation.

We see here a wholly supernatural wisdom by which the angels, in their cosmic function, are "spirits apt for service, whom he sends out when the destined heirs of eternal salvation have need of them". This, as I have said, is how the Epistle to the Hebrews (1. 14) describes them, and all this chapter should be included in the preceding chapter. The greatest commentator of St Thomas, Cajetan (on Ia, Qu. 110, art. 1, ad 2) observes that the order of Providence, to which belongs the intervention of angels in the bodily world, is supernatural, and that, in the order of nature, we could hardly establish this intervention. He goes so far as to say (ad 3) that it would have no reason to exist. The supernatural action of angels in a state of grace is needed in order that the creatures of the visible world should be truly brothers. Thanks to them, even though we fail in our work as priests of creation, even though we do the opposite to what we should, and "are condemned to frustration" and cause it to "groan" (Rom. 8. 20, 22) by a wicked use, it is fundamentally praise of God.

This supernatural action, which for us gives nature its full meaning, is that of freedom. We are far away from the cosmos of the Greeks—and from that of Dante! Behind necessary scientific laws and those incalculable interferences which we call chance, love full of careful attention is at work. To make a machine go when it has been finally adjusted, we do not see why supreme freedom is necessary. But the task which brings the angels into the universe demands the originality of genius: what they work out is a harmony between the eternal destinies of the elect and the new universe they are preparing. The first of these two astonishingly complicated terms involves the constant, unforeseen, action of freedom.

In this task they are infallible, because they know God's plan, and follow it with utter faithfulness, and hence comes the incorruptible, the final character of the fruits of their labour, of the fruits which they gather from the action of beings, its character as rendered eternal. But what remains of the phenomena which in themselves are only results of passing forces? They succeed one another, vanish away, cancel one another. Beneath this phantasmagoria of what in Christian language is called "appearances", a reality, in a relationship with phenomena as mysterious though as certain as the soul with the body, a reality which on the last day will be the "new earth", develops, under the action of the angels, in virtue of an end which is already perfected in the glorified body of Christ, and will be perfected in the "spiritual bodies" of the elect. "To the ancients the world, which is eternal, is sacred. All things, said Thales, are full of Gods: everything is divine—and man's very dignity comes to him through his participation in the cosmos. Christianity, on the contrary, has deprived the world of its sacredness. By making it a created object external to God, it has given it to man, and made possible experimental and practical science" (Jean Lacroix, in *le Monde*, April 12th, 1957).

This is certainly true of the world of "appearances", of phenomena; but it conceals a sacred world. The angels help us to make the world sacred once again, but it is, as we see, in quite a different way from that of the pagans. The pagans made man sacred by participation in the cosmos which they claimed to be eternal; to the Christian this world passes away, and he himself, the "old man", being corruptible, passes with it, but by the sacraments he is made sacred in such a way as to belong to the body of Christ, who "will form this humbled body of ours anew, moulding it into the image of his glorified body, so effective is his power to make all things obey him" (Phil. 3. 21); "inspired, as his glorious power can inspire you" (Col. 1. 11), all his actions, when confirmed to the will of God, cause to emerge from this world—which is not merely no longer made sacred, but is destined to be burnt—the new universe, made sacred by the splendours of Christ, and also through our cooperation with the angels.

psychologist in putting little trust in them. When supernatural faith in its pure form has cured us of that taste for the marvellous which is so harmful to it, accounts such as the one I am about to quote, seem very strange. On the one hand, their authors look very much as though they had the vivid imagination of former days, and made no clear distinction between hallucinations of sight and hearing and real perceptions. But on the other hand our certain knowledge of the angels makes it highly probable that they show themselves sometimes to their friends in some such way. I will confine myself to a single passage: it is from M. Olier.

That holy soul [Mother Agnès de Langeac] made her angel do as she wished. She saw him, spoke familiarly with him, and I remember that, when I left her to go by dangerous roads by night, she gave him to me to help me to get past the danger, and, when I had done so, he said good-bye to me, and went back to the good soul he guarded.

Her good angel, by a special kindness for which I cannot be sufficiently thankful to God, had been given me two days before I heard of her death. Being in the country, very troubled because I had not exhorted some poor peasant I met on the road, suddenly I was thrown on the ground under my horse, without being hurt and, when I wished to remount, I felt myself unable to do so, but was forced to throw myself on my knees and ask pardon of God for my infidelity. Immediately afterwards, having remounted, an angel swooped on me from heaven, like an eagle on its prey, and I heard these words from my good angel: "Pay great reverence to the angel who is beside you; he is one of the greatest that is given to a creature on earth".   (Icard, *Doctrine de M. Olier*, pp. 370–1.)

This new angel, of such high degree, and put at his disposal through the death of Mère Agnès, came to him in this way to help him in his office as superior of the Society of Saint-Sulpice, which had become a heavy burden to him.

It is dangerous for the life of faith if we become too fond

of stories of this kind, which should be regarded with great caution. On the other hand faith is apt to become abstract and theoretical if it does not see the deep probability of such events. The cooking done by the angels in the Franciscan friary, the passages over the flooded road made for St Marie-Madeleine Postel by an angel, the light blow, heard by all, which St Frances of Rome received from her angel when not pleased with her, the place of honour and all the attention demanded of St Peter Canisius by the additional angel he received for his solemn profession, all this has an air of heaven about it. Little things treated like big ones, big like little, and every character treated individually, there is a humour in this which seems fitting to an intervention of citizens of the eternal world in our paltry, yet serious, concerns. "They come very often among Christians without being seen", said St Joan of Arc, "I have often seen them among Christians."

THE ANGEL OF OUR DREAMS

The embarrassment and the charm, both of which are caused us by these delightful stories, arise from the fact that they are too probable. They are too probable both from the heavenly and the earthly point of view. Hence comes our suspicion that they are only projections of dreams on the part of those who received these favours. The profound dreams of the saints are in harmony with the true paradise, because their faith, which is true, inspires even their dreams. We must also hope that for the future the difference between what they think they see and what can be proved may be clarified to meet the demands of the critics.

Our friendship with the angels, however, has no need of signs, for it does not depend on such things. We have seen its basis in strict faith. Yet I must add that it also finds in the depths of our soul something to nourish it and to awake echoes. Deeper than our surface consciousness, a profound awareness of angels responds to our supernatural faith in God's angels. Men's dreams in every age and in every society often include a spreading of wings, a mysterious bird, an angel. This is what Jung calls a "dream archetype", one of those "original images", in which are expressed, deep within us, the common experience of humanity. Like the virgin, or the goddess, and still other symbols, it is an image of the soul itself, which has an obscure awareness of its power to be carried beyond itself. Poets show in the highest degree this awareness of their Psyche, or of their mind which sleeps and awakes, and this experience makes them express their idea of angels.

The danger of using angels as symbols lies in self-sufficiency, and even of preferring the charm of poetic experience to real communication with angels—which is based on faith. On the other hand, if we really live by faith, it is quite right that our devotion to the angels should awaken in us the deep powers of the soul, through which this devotion can become spontaneous and vital. Moreover, there is nothing special we need do for this. If this devotion is an opening of the "heart", instead of being a veneer of feelings and deliberate desires founded on ideas, the psychic energy we possess will be awakened accordingly. Our affinity with the angels must quite naturally favour the integration of our disordered tendencies and develop our friendship with them.

From the standpoint of *true life*, the life of poetry is really vain, if it is content with poetry alone. An awakening in us of the angel idea must in the end be admitted a terrible misfortune, if it is not caused by love of the living God. In the normal course, however, this love must awaken the angel idea, and transfigure our lives even on the level of the senses. In the normal course friendship with the angels flows from within as a delightful glory to our lives.

IN THE FULL DAYLIGHT OF ETERNITY

On the last day this friendship will reveal its true nature, and we shall see what it has meant to us. "The Son of Man will come in his glory, and all the angels with him" (Matt. 25. 31). At their summons the dead will rise. The angels will "gather his elect from the four winds" (Matt. 24. 30; 1 Thess. 4. 16). Then they will be the reapers who separate the good seed from the tares (Matt. 13. 40–1).

In doing this they are doing the work, which is always theirs, of preparing for God's coming, of making men ready for union with God. For what we call the "last day" will be the first of full life.

The great gothic story of St Michael weighing the souls in a balance is not scriptural, but comes from the early days of ancient Egypt: Anubis held the balance, Cairis presided over the judgement. It also comes from Greece, where Mercury weighed souls in the presence of Apollo. It expresses in a striking image the idea of a just judgement. Yet it is too simple. All the angels and all the saints will take part in the judgement, and they will be present both as judges and as judged. This judgement will really be the manifestation of that order which is being worked out now and throughout the whole of time, amid the variety of all actions, in the mystery of hearts. Everyone of our acts judges us; it plays its part in changing us in ourselves, and this for eternity. The judgement will be the manifestation of all that results from this. Undoubtedly we are not sufficiently convinced of the Kingdom of God, of the new earth, of the order of charity, which already exists and is victorious in Christ, in his angels, and in the blessed. What happens at the last day should be regarded rather as our actual possession of that City than as a waiting for its future coming. We may put it by saying this should be described in the dimension of height rather than in the horizontal perspective of the future.

Awareness of this actual possession makes us understand from within the realities of the kingdom of God, which puzzle us when we try to grasp them from without. With regard to the Second Coming this helps us to understand the strange words of St Paul: "You have been told that we shall sit in judgement on angels" (1 Cor. 6. 3). Through participation in the exaltation of Christ above the angelic orders, through the vision in God of the accomplishment of salvation, we shall understand the part which the angels will have played, we shall do them justice wondering at them and glorifying them with the sovereign Judge. This "judgement" of angels, as far as the good angels are concerned, can only be the burst of praise following perfect understanding of their work, which eternal Truth will cause.

Then all creation will be a perfect harmony of the new heaven, the new earth, the angelic orders and risen men. At present the material creation "groans in a common travail"; "condemned to frustration", it hopes to be "set free from the tyranny of corruption, to share in the glorious freedom of God's sons" (Rom. 8. 18, 22). St Paul speaks of "glorious freedom". Our constant movement here below always makes us conceive, by contrast, God's stability as inactive. The glory of God will certainly hold risen men captive after the Second Coming, as it now holds captive the angels and the souls of the blessed. But in giving them to themselves and in taking them infinitely beyond themselves, it leaves them immense freedom in regard to all that is not God. We are right to picture paradise as a place of peace, but it will surely seem to us a place of frantic activity compared to the most intense activities of this world. We should think of the music and dancing in the new earth, beneath the new skies—of all that will be done to show their friendship by the countless angels and all the blessed, active and resplendent with their risen bodies, and with their souls open to one another, and giving joy to all.

It may be asked what is left for the angels to do, when they have finished their works of kindness, and there is no more suffering to relieve. To "place his kingship in the hands of God", Christ will first have "to dispossess every other sort of rule, authority and power" (1 Cor. 15. 24), and this it is tempting to explain as meaning that he will put an end to their duties—presumably in their present form. But surely those who give enlightenment to one another will also have wonderful works to perform among the saints (Ia, Qu. 108, art. 7). To know what these will be we should have to know how our glorious liberty will be employed. All this we can only find out when the time comes—what our eyes will see in God's light, what our ears will hear, what our hands will fashion, where our steps will take us, and what thoughts will rise in our hearts. God has only told us what we need to know in order to advance in his paths. Where they will lead us will be certainly a wonderful surprise, yet undoubtedly we shall have a work to do there, to which God destines us, and for which he counts upon us, and it is probable, from what we know of the laws of his kingdom, that we shall be fellow workers there with the angels. Perfect friendship can only mean for these latter the fullest and most intense life. Our friends, the angels, will help us to perform our duties in eternity.

So let us now at the present time rejoice exceedingly, through our faith, in union with the mysterious choir of angels.

SELECT BIBLIOGRAPHY

ARMSTRONG, A. H.: *Architecture of the Intelligible Universe in the Philosophy of Plotinus*, Oxford and New York, Oxford Univ. Press, 1940; *Plotinus*, London, Allen and Unwin, New York, Macmillan, 1953.

BRUNO DE JÉSUS-MARIE, editor: *Satan*, London and New York, Sheed and Ward, 1952.

COLLINS, J. D.: *Thomistic Philosophy of the Angels*, Washington, Catholic Univ. of America Press, 1957.

COPLESTON, F., S.J.: *History of Philosophy*, Volume 2, London, Burns Oates, and Westminster, Md, Newman Press, 1950.

DANIÉLOU, J., S.J.: *Advent*, London and New York, Sheed and Ward, 1956.

DANTE: *Divine Comedy: being the Vision of Dante Alighieri*, ed. H. F. Cary, Oxford and New York, Oxford Univ. Press, 1910.

DENIS (Dionysius) the Areopagite: *Celestial and Ecclesiastical Hierarchy*, trans. J. Parker, London, Skeffington, 1894.

FARRELL, Walter, O.P.: *A Companion to the Summa*, Vol. 1, London and New York, Sheed and Ward, 1945.

HENRY, A. M., O.P.: editor: *God and His Creation*, Volume 2 of Theology Library, Cork, Mercier Press and Chicago, Fides, 1955.

MURPHY, W. B., O.P.: *God and His Creation*, Dubuque, Priory Press, 1958.

SCHEEBEN, Matthias J.: *Mysteries of Christianity*, St Louis, Herder, 1946.

VONIER, Dom Anscar: *The Angels*, reprinted in *The Teaching of the Catholic Church*, London, Burns Oates, and New York, Macmillan, 1949; *The Human Soul*, reprinted in *The Collected Works*, Volume 3, London, Burns Oates, and Westminster, Md, Newman Press, 1953.

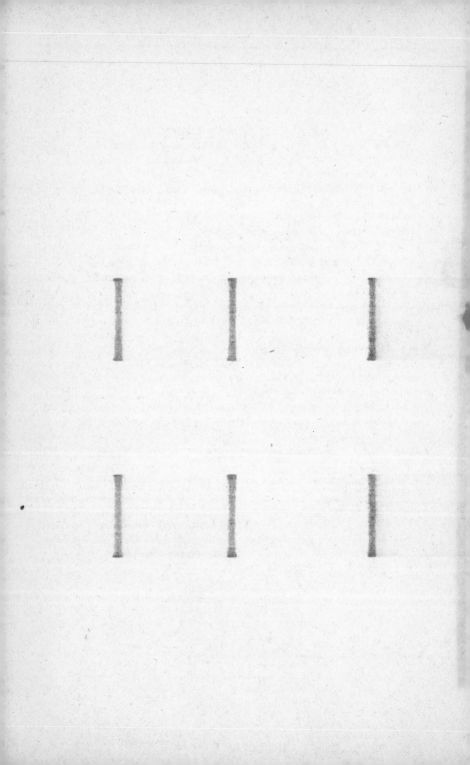

CHAPTER VI

OUR FRIENDSHIP WITH
THE ANGELS

Being made "fit to share the light which saints inherit" (Col. 1. 12), we share it too with the angels, for saints and angels dwell together in heaven. Clement of Alexandria wrote: "You will dance with the angels around God, the uncreated, imperishable, and truly one." St Antony, in the words attributed to him by St Athanasius, asserted—and the belief is continuous from the time of the Fathers—that we are destined to take the places left empty among the angels by the fall of the devils. We have seen that, in the eyes of St Bernard, this is the chief cause of the eagerness with which the good angels seek to ensure that we fulfil our destinies. "There are not four cities," St Augustine insists, "two of the angels and two of men, but only two cities or societies, one made up of the good, the other of the wicked, whether men or angels" (*City of God*, Bk. 12, Chapter 1). This belief can in no way be discredited by the inference which it appears we should draw from a false reading of our Lord's words: "Those who are found worthy to attain that other world, and resurrection from the dead ... will be as the angels in heaven are" (Luke 20. 35–6)—understanding this resemblance as an equality (the Vulgate translates: *aequales angelis in coelis*). However this may be, certainly the communication of God's life in the full brightness of his glory draws together all those who enjoy it, whether angels or men, so closely that the difference of their natures is overcome. The degrees in Paradise are those of glory, and undoubtedly human beings can be raised to the highest degree, for the Blessed Virgin reigns over all the angels. Moreover St Thomas found a suspicion of heresy in the opinion that men could never do more than form an order lower than that of the angels (*2 Sent*. dist. 9, art. 8).

It was God's "loving design, centred in Christ, to give history its fulfilment by resuming everything in him, all that is in heaven, all that is on earth, summed up in him" (Ephes. 1. 10). The angels and ourselves are eternally "fellow servants" (Apoc. 19. 10; 22. 9). God's grace has "raised us up too, enthroned us too above the heavens, in Christ Jesus" (Ephes. 2. 6), and from this earth we approach "thousands upon thousands of angels" (Hebr. 12. 22). "There is joy among them over one sinner that repents" (Luke 15. 10), and goes to join them. "Hasten", cries St Gregory to us, "to have yourselves inscribed in the heavenly court of the angels."

How are we to answer the help which in their friendship they offer us? We think at once of devotion, honour, love, and we are right. Yet these are valueless if they do not flow from a life conforming itself as far as possible to that of our friends in heaven.

THE ANGELIC LIFE

Such conformity must be understood in a deeper sense than the activity of the moral virtues by which we try to imitate them. It consists in a complete change of our very being, by means of grace, which in their eyes give us a likeness to their orders of being. Radically baptism makes us shine with a brightness at which St Ambrose tells us the angels marvel (*De Sacramentis* 4, 2, 5). The priestly character and the grace it confers make priests like to that condition of supernatural mediators and messengers from God to men, which is the condition of the angels. The monastic state in particular was called in the early days of Christianity, and is still called in the eastern Churches, "the angelic life": its very nature is to develop to the full the grace of baptism, so that it may form here on earth, so far as possible, an anticipation of the eschatological "new earth". When the contemplative life is genuine, it changes him who adopts it, making his mind reach, says St Thomas, "the form of unity, which is that of the angels" (IIa IIae, Qu. 180, art. 6 ad 2).

All this needs fuller explanation, as we are less familiar with it today. It certainly lies at a deeper level than the moral life and at least requires for its perfection an activity of virtue which must now be called "angelic".

The chief characteristic of it is integrity. It goes without saying that man, complex as he is, can lay no claim to that of the angels, but it is by tending towards the integration with himself of all that is outside him, that he enters to some extent into union with these things. The ancients insisted on this. Man, said St Gregory, "is, so to speak, dissipated outside himself, and he can no longer see the splendours of his heavenly country". And St Thomas: "He is distracted by the sensible things which absorb him." Plainly it is God's love, the law of the heavenly city, which must gradually make him one. This must establish its rule in his "heart", in the Biblical sense of the word, correct his spirit, inspire all his powers, and thus influence him in the depths of his soul.

When we hear of imitation of the holy angels as a means to the necessary integration of the anarchic elements of our microcosm, in order to spread abroad love, we obviously run no risk of worship of the angels: indeed such imitation is enjoined by the state of incarnation and weakness for which it must provide a remedy.

Communion with the angels stimulates all the virtues. The

saints have shown this more particularly for some virtues. *Religion:* these "fellow servants" sing the glory of God, stir us to worship, the celebration of which here on earth is, as I have said, a participation in their liturgy. *Mercy:* being ministers to us of the divine mercy, they press us to devote ourselves to effective works of sympathy and love. St John Chrysostom writes: "They run from all sides. It is the office of an angel to do all for the salvation of our brethren." *Chastity:* the meaning of the new "earth" at the end of the world must be explained if we are to understand how it is an "angelic" virtue. Because for this meaning there has been substituted in the modern world sentimentality (often made worse by a suspicious hatred of the flesh), this expression has become queer and even false. The traditional awe of virginity is caused by its connection with the world in which we shall be like the angels, and where there is no marrying and giving in marriage (Matt. 22. 30). The complex of virtues and gifts which makes up *poverty:* the fact of our belonging to such a world renders the world of angels with which we are surrounded so real through hope, that we like to reduce to bare necessity our use of perishable goods. *Penitence:* through spiritual freedom we turn our acceptance of suffering, and indeed of all mortification, into a true repentance, that is, conduct inspired by awareness of what lies beyond our present feebleness.

The need to integrate ourselves little by little leads us towards what has been called, following St Thomas, the "mixed" life of contemplation and activity. In its perfect state this is the life of the angels. For we understand it in a wholly superficial way if we think of it as a succession of periods of contemplation and of activity. St Ignatius of Loyola expressed its true nature when he told Ribadeneira of his wish "to be like the angels in not letting himself be distracted by any of his occupations, just as the angels do not cease to see God and rejoice in him". Unfortunately, it can only mean for us a desire and a tendency to this: we do not see God, as the angels do, and the service of our neighbour distracts us with a multitude of perishable things. We should have a very false notion of the angels if we supposed that we possessed an imaginary unity, when in fact we are divided between an idea of God, hopeless to maintain when we are active and spend our psychic energy, and that activity which we cannot then attend to as is necessary. Wise imitation of the angels takes different forms in accordance with our vocation. Every vocation implies a tendency towards rest in God, towards simplication of the love of the "heart" with which we look to him, that is, towards contemplation. But active natures will only be able to look with a certain steadiness, if they spend themselves in their practical services. Apart from exceptional graces or works which are more or less automatic and leave their minds free, they will not, like angels, have their period of contemplation during their other activity (except perhaps sudden illuminations); they are like the angels in so far as this activity is derived from the actual fullness of their love, and it is this which keeps them from becoming disturbed by their practical good works. At the other extreme "pure contemplatives" have scarcely any external occupations which turn aside their loving attention to God. Their whole being must be changed so effectively by the likeness they achieve to the supernatural realities which they contemplate, that Christ "renews in them all his mystery", the mystery of the salvation of the world, and however secretly men join in it, the communion of saints gives them more scope for fraternal charity. "Pure contemplatives" are like the angels by the completeness of the gift they make to God. Their service of man, like that of the angels, cannot be seen (though here there is much danger of self-deception). Vocations to the "mixed" life are most perfectly angelic, if the contemplation and the active service do not spoil one another. That they may be in harmony, they must obviously have the same aim; the active service must be able, ordinarily, to be contemplative. For this it must consist in the transmission to others of God's Truth, or, better, of his *epiphany*. The vocation to the "mixed" life is an appeal to this activity among the angels, who, according to St Gregory, contemplate God's face in the souls that God entrusts to them, and turn towards the divine face in virtue of the brightness they receive from it and transmit.

DEVOTION TO THE ANGELS

A life which is in harmony with our friends in heaven gives depth to our devotion for them, and to the veneration we pay them. In return this devotion and veneration are the form usually taken by the friendship with which we reply to theirs. There is danger of such devotion becoming superficial, of only consisting of ideas, feelings and such actions as the celebration of one of their feasts, or a pilgrimage to some sanctuary like Mont Saint-Michel. But the giving of "worship in spirit and in truth" involves essentially—this cannot be sufficiently emphasized—a renewal of heart and an effective tendency towards unity of our whole being through love of God, on which I have just insisted.

As to our veneration of them, I need hardly mention that it cannot be the kind of worship we pay to God, but only subordinate to this.[1] Usually at the present day there is no danger of exaggeration, though this was not always the case. We can understand better why St Paul seems to underrate the good angels, when we find that a local Council at Laodicea in Phrygia between 343 and 381 was obliged to condemn Christians who "leave the Church of God and turn away from it, giving themselves up in honour of the angels to a masked idolatry". Certain fathers, such as Eusebius, or Theodoret, had also to stop the veneration paid to angels. Now it is necessary, rather, to revive it. Certainly, as a result of the

[1] See M.-D. Philippe, O.P., *The Worship of God*, in this series.

present study, we can see their importance in introducing us to the invisible world and, in contrast with this, the little devotion that is usually paid them.

The veneration we should give them depends entirely on the fact that their work is always to dispose us for fuller and more direct union with God. This is by no means in contradiction with the *negation* of everything created which is required for the mystic union. This latter requirement is expressed again and again, from one generation to the next, as, for instance, by Angelus Silesius: "Away from here, Archangels, away. Seraphim! I wish for nothing from you, for the sight of you is vain! I shall satisfy fully the hunger I endure, in the uncreated depths of pure deity."

To describe the devotion we should normally offer to the angels, it is best to meditate on the well-known passage in which St Bernard expresses the devotion we should pay to our guardian angel. Let us apply to all our friends in all the hierarchies the dispositions that he would instil into us.

"He has given charge to his angels concerning thee, to watch over thee wherever thou goest" (Ps. 90). What reverence, love and confidence these words should inspire in you! Reverence for the presence of your angel, love for his goodness, confidence in his protection.... Whatever may be your dwelling-place, whatever the corner to which you withdraw, have the greatest reverence for your angel. Would you dare to do in his presence what you would not do in my presence? Do you doubt his presence, because you do not see him?...

That you may have confidence in the angels, my brethren, constantly keep in company, by means of your thoughts and devout prayers, with those who are always at hand to guard and console you....

Let us cause the angels to exult with joy, by showing them that we are not only converted, but that we advance in virtue, practising the virtues which are most dear to them: modesty, chastity, poverty, the spirit of prayer, and above all charity in union and peace.

THE FIORETTI OF THE ANGELS

There can, and therefore must, exist mutual friendship between the angels and ourselves. Usually it develops without our realizing it, yet involving inspirations, fortunate encounters, in which we can hardly help recognizing the care they have for us. They are full of kindness. They seem to delight in arranging their interventions in a way which is as hidden as it is undeniable. Do we not find this in many passages of Scripture? Tobias is an obvious example, and the morning of the resurrection. To roll away the stone from the tomb one of them appeared like lightning: "his face shone like lightning", and the guards were terrified (Matt. 28. 2). When the women, early in the morning, stooped down in the tomb, two "men" in shining garments stood by them. The women, too, were frightened, but the "men" explained to them with a wonderful impressiveness: "Why are you seeking one who is alive, here among the dead? He is not here, he has risen again" (Luke 24. 4 following). They disappeared when Peter and John also arrived. They were again present to receive the second visit of Mary Magdalen, like two men, in their simple white garments. Mary bent down weeping, and when, with her eyes full of tears, she saw them, she spoke sadly with them as though they were intruders (John 20. 11 following).

These different kinds of behaviour on the part of the angels, in their visible appearances in Scripture, certainly deserved to be studied, to make us familiar with their ways. It would be valuable to have a *Fioretti*, a collection of the occasions on which they have intervened, when there is good evidence for it, as shown in the lives of many holy persons. It would indeed be immensely difficult to decide on this evidence, and often impossible to make a critical examination. Very often the visions are imaginary, and the theologian agrees with the